AF328759

CREATING
VALUE

EMPOWERING PEOPLE FOR
SUSTAINABLE SUCCESS THAT BENEFITS
EMPLOYEES, CUSTOMERS, AND OWNERS

CREATING VALUE

JOHN RIZZO
with TOM EHRENFELD

WILEY

Published by John Wiley & Sons, Inc., Hoboken, New Jersey.

Published simultaneously in Canada.

Library of Congress Cataloging-in-Publication Data is Available:

ISBN 9781394342839 (Cloth)
ISBN 9781394342846 (ePub)
ISBN 9781394342853 (ePDF)

Cover Design: Wiley
Cover Image: © BlackSalmon/Getty Images

Printed and bound by CPI Group (UK) Ltd, Croydon CR0 4YY

C9781394342839_150925

*To everyone who participated in
workshops with me, endeavoring to improve*

Contents

Acknowledgments

This book represents the culmination of a journey that began more than 30 years ago on a factory floor in Syracuse, New York. It would not have been possible without the wisdom, guidance, and support of countless individuals who have shaped my understanding of how to create enduring value.

First and foremost, I owe an immeasurable debt to my mentors, who introduced me to the principles and practices of continuous improvement. Chihiro Nakao, whose penetrating insights and unyielding standards taught me to see waste where others saw normal operations. Art Byrne, who taught me humility and demonstrated how leadership commitment transforms organizations and nearly threw me off a chairlift when I proudly described my "vendor-managed inventory" solution. Yoshiki Iwata, who showed me the power of simplicity and focus. Bill Moffitt, who told me to "listen to the operator and move the machine six inches," forever changing my perspective on where wisdom resides in organizations. Bob Pentland, who refused to give me formulas and instead made me learn through struggle and discovery. Jim Cutler, whose patience and practical approach helped me translate lofty principles into everyday practice.

John Fitzgibbons, chair of Basin and Talus Holding companies, who showed me what leadership is in a fast-changing, entrepreneurial environment.

I want to thank Julia Rizzo, who, after years of listening to heroic stories from the people who do the work, helped me put it all down on paper.

I am profoundly grateful to the thousands of workers, supervisors, managers, and executives who participated in workshops with me over the decades. Your willingness to question established practices, experiment with new approaches, and share both successes and failures has been the true foundation of everything I've learned. Special thanks to the machine operator at Crouse-Hinds who had the courage to speak up about moving that machine, setting me on this path.

To my colleagues at Moffitt Consultants, especially Rick Jeffrey, Brett Jaffe, and Mark Hamel, who shared this journey with me. Thank you for your partnership, challenge, and support. The collaborative learning we experienced together expanded my horizons far beyond what I could have discovered alone.

I am grateful to the board members and investors who believed in this approach even when it seemed counter to conventional wisdom. Your willingness to focus on long-term value creation rather than short-term extraction made transformations possible.

Thank you to all those who contributed to the creation of this book: acclaimed editor Tom Ehrenfeld, who helped sharpen my thinking and clarify my expression; those who provided feedback on early drafts; and the team who managed production and distribution.

To my family, who endured my frequent absences during workshops and transformations, and who patiently listened as I excitedly described the latest breakthrough in setup reduction or material replenishment systems, your love and support made everything possible.

Finally, my deepest appreciation goes to the frontline workers in organizations around the world. You are the true heroes of this story. Your insights, creativity, and commitment to improvement demonstrate daily that the most valuable asset in any organization is its people. This book is ultimately a testament to what becomes possible when we honor your wisdom and create environments where everyone can contribute to creating value.

Preface

In the relentless pursuit of quarterly profits and short-term gains, many organizations have lost sight of what truly creates enduring value. Today's business landscape is increasingly dominated by approaches that extract value rather than create it, where financial engineering trumps operational excellence, where employees are seen as costs to be minimized rather than assets to be developed, and where customers are viewed as transactions rather than relationships.

This book offers a different path forward.

For more than 30 years, I've had the privilege of witnessing and participating in transformations that have created billions of dollars in value across diverse industries—not through financial manipulation or exploitative practices, but through a comprehensive approach that respects and develops people while relentlessly improving processes. The results speak for themselves: dramatic improvements in quality, delivery times slashed from months to days, safety incidents reduced by 80 percent or more, and profits that consistently outperform industry averages.

What you'll find in these pages isn't just theory, but proven practice distilled from over 1,000 workshops and dozens of organizational transformations. From manufacturing men's suits to processing insurance claims, from producing rocket fuel to managing luxury apartment complexes, the principles and approaches shared have demonstrated their universal applicability.

The holistic business system described isn't simply another set of tools or techniques to be mechanically implemented. It represents a fundamentally different way of thinking about work, people, and value creation. At its core lies a simple yet profound approach: being present where work happens, observing with open eyes, and truly listening to those who do the work.

This journey begins with that pivotal moment at Crouse-Hinds when a machine operator suggested moving equipment just six inches to improve his work. That small act of listening and responding set in motion what would become a career-long commitment to this way of creating value. The lessons learned from that moment and countless others since then have shaped my understanding of what makes organizations truly excellent.

Whether you lead a global enterprise or a small team, whether you work in manufacturing, healthcare, technology, or services, the principles in this book apply. The system works everywhere because it addresses fundamental human and organizational dynamics that transcend industry boundaries.

My hope is that this book will inspire you to reconsider conventional management practices and embrace a more sustainable, humane, and ultimately profitable approach to business. The path I describe isn't always easy, but the rewards—for employees, customers, shareholders, and society—are immense.

The choice is yours. Will you be lured by the path of value extraction, or will you commit to creating value that benefits all stakeholders? The journey toward operational excellence begins with the decision to be present, to observe, and to listen. Everything else follows from there.

Chapter 1

Move the Machine Six Inches

"Listen to the machine operator and move the machine six inches," my mentor, Bill Moffitt, who was coaching me in a team improvement workshop, advised me.

My colleagues and I were gathered on the factory floor of the Crouse-Hinds Company on a Monday morning in Syracuse, New York. Crouse-Hinds (then a part of Cooper Industries, now a subsidiary of Eaton Corporation) is a leading manufacturer of electrical equipment, specializing in products designed to withstand hazardous and harsh conditions.

The stakes are high when manufacturing this type of equipment. When a worker is doing electrical installation on an offshore drilling rig in the Gulf of Mexico, for example, an explosion-proof electrical enclosure can mean the difference between a straightforward day on the job and a catastrophic explosion.

On this cold and snowy Syracuse day in 1993, we were gathered to conduct a team improvement workshop. Based on lessons learned by our mentor from Toyota, this workshop was the first of its kind at Cooper Industries. The team consisted of production workers, union officials, supervisors, and management. It is fair to say that everyone in attendance was apprehensive. The members of the team represented a diverse array of disparate—or even competing—interests and agendas.

The goal of that 1993 event was to create *flow*. Flow is a term that describes any work in process that moves forward without pausing and each piece is completed individually rather than in a batch. Prior to this event, the manufacturing equipment on the factory floor was divided into distinct functional departments. The divisions between the functional departments had prevented work from flowing between stations without conveyance or other delays.

During this workshop, the team brought all the workers together to create a unit called a *cell*. This reconfigured way of working reduced lead times by shortening the distance the parts had to travel, as well as reducing the amount of time the parts spent "sitting around."

The potential benefits of the new cell were significant. By eliminating the siloed functional departments and creating cells, we enabled faster delivery, immediate identification of quality issues, lower cost from less handling, and less inventory.

Making these changes produced human and organizational benefits that extended far beyond the immediate logistic—and even financial—advantages created by moving equipment. Culturally, we were making it clear in the moment that we were serious about change—and that every person involved was empowered to be change agents. Workshops have a bias for action, meaning there is little to no delay between decision-making, planning, and implementation. When we made the decision to create the cells, we got them up and running in the same week.

Implementing the new structure was simple but not easy. Moving multi-ton manufacturing equipment to create cells is an intensive process. Due to the size and weight of the equipment, we needed to bring in an outside contractor—a "rigger"—to make the move. Demonstrating our bias for action, we hired the rigger and moved the equipment on the third day of the weeklong workshop. Improvements that can be made in real time often yield the best outcomes.

By the end of the third day, the rigger had repositioned the machines. When we came in the morning after we moved the equipment and asked the machine operators for their feedback on the new layout, one worker said, "If this machine was turned six inches, I wouldn't have to walk an extra step. I could just turn and reach."

My initial thought was about the expenditure needed to rehire the rigger to move the machine a scant six inches, adding time and cost to the process. And yet my coach, Bill Moffitt, said something that permanently opened my eyes. He looked at me and said, "Listen to the operator. Move the equipment six inches." I trusted Bill to do so, and so we reluctantly brought the riggers back and repositioned the equipment.

And this operator eventually said, "My gosh, they actually listened to me and did what was best!" His conviction made my job easier moving forward. While the union was initially suspicious of what we were doing, that simple act got the ball rolling in terms of building trust and mutual respect. Change driven by the people who do the work proved to be more successful than the traditional "top-down" manufacturing management approach. We got to the point where the union started suggesting areas of improvement and volunteering to participate in workshops.

In that instant, Bill Moffitt helped me understand the enduring value of listening to the people who are doing the work and acting on it swiftly. I truly do not know where my career would be today if we hadn't moved that piece of equipment six inches and made that operator's job a little better, while simultaneously making delivery to the customer a little faster.

By immediately acting—agreeing simply to move the equipment in that moment—we sent a key message not just in the moment, but for the long term, responding to and validating what this operator shared based on his years of experience.

That was the start of my continuous improvement journey. That event laid the seeds for the convictions that have guided me for decades. At that moment, on the factory floor, we saw what was going on, listened to the operator, and made improvements.

This simple interaction marked the start of the continuous improvement journey at Crouse-Hinds. We earned buy-in from the operators almost immediately. Notably, the operator who suggested moving the equipment six inches was a union steward. He saw that the continuous improvement team observed the work being done, sought his input, and took his feedback seriously. He then told his colleagues in the union to give it a try. There was little written at the time about this improvement process, and he put his trust in us based on our actions.

Over the coming months and years, we would radically transform how this producer of electrical construction materials organized the way they made their products, in a way that would serve their customers far more powerfully and productively than they had before. We eliminated their archaic method of breaking work down into functional departments (like machining, wash, assembly, warehousing, and more), and created eight business units that were organized by value stream instead. Now each business unit incorporates everything needed to get a product to a customer—including administrative functions such as engineering, purchasing, and accounting—that were previously siloed. Doing so allowed us to produce items in a state of flow where work traveled seamlessly from raw materials to a finished product.

This huge change delivered benefits far beyond the cost savings from having pieces in process sitting around waiting to be passed to the next step. We reduced the many costs associated with waiting, overproduction of parts, overprocessing of materials, excessive inventory, and more. We would now have positive pressure on fixing problems as they occurred. In addition, implementing flow produced enormous gains in on-time delivery and quality, because, as quality issues emerged, workers would discover and immediately resolve the source of the defect then and there.

From such small gains we cumulatively garnered significant achievements. Over time, we reduced inventory levels by 50 percent, reduced operating costs by 15 percent, reduced defects by 80 percent, and set new records for customer service with an on-time delivery mark of 100 percent. Filtering out all the excessive inventory, work, and capital from how we made things, coupled with greater customer satisfaction, improved cash flow for the business by more than $30 million.

That moment represented more than the start of the journey of continuous improvement for Crouse-Hinds. That workshop and all the beliefs embedded in it (whether known or simply suggested at the time) generated foundational ideas that have informed my entire career. That was the first time I deeply understood the importance of *being present, seeing the work being done, and listening to the people doing the work.*

Sure, we reaped the expected operational benefits, and the cell ended up reducing lead times by several weeks by producing parts in one-piece flow versus moving large batches between different departments. Our customers were delighted by our ability to serve them faster and more flexibly. But more than that, I discovered enduring and repeatable cultural lessons that have guided me and my colleagues over a range of successful turnarounds and breakthrough transformations.

Over the last 30 years I have led or participated in more than 1,000 workshops through my work as an executive, an investor, or a consultant with Moffitt, helping implement a better way. I've seen this approach improve the work in hospitals and mattress retailers, in temporary medical staffing firms and laboratory animal science companies. I've seen it boost the quality, on-time delivery, service, and cost structure of companies that make everything from men's suits to steel doors to rocket fuel to drywall. I've seen this apply in every type of company and firm; I know that it works as effectively at a global manufacturing company as it does in a small museum, zoo, governmental agency, or nonprofit. I don't know where my career would be today if it wasn't for moving that piece of equipment six inches.

My colleagues and I call this approach a "holistic business system," and I'm a firm believer that following this way of creating value represents a better way for companies to succeed today.

In recent years, companies have increasingly turned to short-term opportunistic strategies based on leveraging capital, bullying customers, and exploiting technical advantage for growth. This prevalent approach seeks ways to extract value quickly from companies and organizations by selling assets and holding customers captive. This approach represents a way of business that disrespects employees and customers, delivers a limited product or service to customers, and proves itself unsustainable over time.

We see this in the triumph of some private equity firms that profit from framing companies as static agglomerations of assets to be purchased and then sold piecemeal, with no vision of the greater whole. Debt is a neutral tool employed to maximize transactional values, and little care is paid to the long-term viability and health of the enterprise. All the profit is generated by the deal, and none of it is contingent on boosting the long-term health—and profit—of the venture. This impatient, transactional, short-term process does little to nothing to increase the health and vitality of healthy businesses and operates largely as a massive transfer of wealth into a small, concentrated set of financiers.

Employees in this way of doing business are seen as expenses to be cut, impersonal costs that are fungible and expendable. Loyalty and expertise are rarely valued. The value of learning and growth is profoundly discounted.

Through my work helping more than 50 companies and organizations transform I've learned that a better way is possible. Many companies (and nonprofit organizations) today are poised to achieve their strategic objectives and experience healthy growth by providing exceptional products or services, and doing so in an enduring and inclusive way that creates value for employees, customers, stakeholders, and society at large.

This approach applies equally to retail and service businesses as it does to small manufacturers making basement doors and, of course, to large multinational corporations. I've learned this through my work with many such organizations over the past three decades, helping them improve the quality of their earnings while preserving and generating stable work for loyal employees year after year. Such quiet, consistent performers churn out profits and generate good jobs for loyal employees year after year.

Internally, my peers and I have codified these principles as a "holistic business system," a comprehensive business system of continuous improvement that serves people, employees, and organizations. This approach has created billions in value for all involved by dramatically eliminating the waste that can be found in existing organizations. This system unlocks value by empowering the people who do the work to improve the work, and it taps into a more focused and productive organization to deliver superior value to customers in a way that improves consistently over time.

THE BUILDING BLOCKS OF CREATING VALUE

A handful of core values animates this framework: fundamentals such as being present, seeing the work being done (at the workplace itself), showing respect by listening to the people doing the work, acknowledging their contributions, and valuing their opinions. These building blocks support and reinforce each other in a dynamic system where value compounds over time.

This approach runs contrary to many accepted truths about how to compete in today's economy, including a firm commitment to respecting the input of those who do the work, focusing relentlessly on creating and delivering more value to customers over time, and achieving success through consistent internal improvement, rather than gaming the system or gambling recklessly with capital. This business system is the result of my lifelong journey with business transformations and continuous improvement.

This hands-on business system has a bias for action in the service of eliminating waste—to serve and deliver eternally growing value to customers. And while improving the processes by which organizations deliver value to customers naturally reduces cost, the primary benefits are that it creates the best possible quality, delivery, and service to create value for employees, customers, stakeholders, and society. And it has paid off for us consistently in myriad companies in a wide range of industries over time, resulting in billions of dollars in value creation. Applying these insights will enable you to unleash dramatic value by empowering your people in any company, anywhere.

I do not profess to be an expert in Lean, Six Sigma, Toyota Production System, Danaher, or Wiremold. However, I have learned greatly from each of them. I have been fortunate to have great teachers and mentors, including Chihiro Nakao, Art Bryne, Yoshiki Iwata, Bill Moffitt, Bob Pentland, and Jim Cutler. However, the best teacher of all has been the workplace itself and the people who do the work. All the stories, experiences, and lessons in this book contribute to this model.

This business system is not the Toyota Production System or Lean. It is a collection of what I have learned over many years from many teachers, businesses, and organizations. It's about developing people. It's about observing, listening, and making improvements. It's about eliminating waste to optimize quality, delivery, service, and cost structure. The system is hands-on with a bias for action. It is not a cost-reduction project, although process improvement process may result in cost reduction. It is about having the best possible quality, delivery, and service to create value for employees, customers, stakeholders, and society. It is applicable to any industry or organization. I have been involved with many transformations, and without the whole system, I have never seen breakthrough transformation and real value creation.

THE LEGACY OF QUALITY

In all these organizations, we have seen irrefutable proof that *quality is the engine of growth*. And that internal, built-in excellence eventually manifests as superior performance in the marketplace. Enduring success is not about gaming the system; it's about becoming world-class to play the game successfully. Superior processes inevitably produce superior results in every company and organization.

These building blocks have roots in a system of production, which was named by a team of researchers from MIT after years of study into the Toyota Production System (TPS). These researchers, including authors Jim Womack and Dan Jones, identified the dynamics of the approach that allowed Toyota to produce cars far more cheaply, faster, and simultaneously with higher quality (measured by far fewer defects) than its global competitors—and which over decades enabled the company to be the global leader in the number of vehicles produced. Since the research team shared this approach, organizations throughout the world have adopted some form of quality informed by the Toyota Production System, as a means of eliminating waste, boosting quality, and spreading a structured approach to problem-solving and learning.

Continuous improvement today is often seen as a "buzzy" phrase associated with cost-cutting and Japanese management. Many excellent books, like Jeff Liker's *The Toyota Way* and Jim Womack and Dan Jones's *Lean Thinking*, have shared the core ideas in a powerful and actionable manner. And many large companies have embarked on a path with varying degrees of success and commitment. GE under Larry Culp represents a fascinating case of a global leader practicing this extensively at every corner of the organization.

Despite this progress, continuous improvement today has suffered from its success. Leading experts spend too much time feuding over whose trademarked approach has the most "authentic" lineage to Japanese sensei, while consultancies invest deeply in producing thin-sliced intellectual products as a means of luring potential clients. Most books about continuous improvement and quality focus narrowly on producing better process numbers while losing sight of vital context, such as consistently boosting quality, delivery, and service while serving loyal employees and customers.

Part of the problem is that the core practices should be easy to follow, and yet they are rarely followed consistently today. The key practices run counter to the prevailing business mindset that taps impatient capital, exploits workers, thinks only in the short term, and sees strategy as a tactical pursuit of temporary monopolies and captive customers. Finally, it has all too often been presented as an end, a noble quest to attain perfection without clear business outcomes. This book intends to clearly establish a link between outstanding process excellence and enduring success in the marketplace.

Creating Value reveals how pursuing excellence leads to outstanding business results that accrue and endure over years. It will help business leaders dramatically boost employee participation and agency, while steadily increasing profits and boosting enterprise value, leading to widely shared creation of value.

Creating Value shares compelling proof that this approach creates unlimited value in virtually any organization imaginable. I define value as what is important to the recipient. While this may vary by individual, I have found these to be of highest importance and fall into three categories:

What's important to the **customer**?

- Quality
- On-time delivery of a product or service
- Reasonable cost

What's important to **employees**?

- Clear expectations and responsibilities/standard work
- Training and resources necessary to be successful
- Safe and decent work environment
- Fair compensation

What's important to **stakeholders**?

- Provide exceptional products or services
- Financially effective

If we improve people lives with exceptional products, services, and jobs, *society* is served. And how do we create what is important to customers, employees, and stakeholders? We utilize a version of this holistic business system.

This book is set apart by the depth and variety of authentic stories about improvement activities—real-world examples of people doing the work and making improvements. You will learn about creating value not from generic descriptions or mundane history lessons but from actual workshops, the way I did.

Above all, this approach taps the power of a holistic business system. You will learn how companies adopted a comprehensive management approach focused on continuous improvement and operational excellence, one that offers a dynamic way to engage every employee in delivering more value to the customer. You will understand how this approach strategically targets waste reduction through value stream analysis, daily improvement efforts, and workshop teams, implementing fundamental principles while ensuring workplace organization and accountability.

You will also learn the primary importance of empowering people. The system promotes and fosters a culture where improvement emerges from the insights of the employees doing the work. This begins with a clear mandate to respect the safety of our workers above all, but extends far beyond the notion that the input of each individual matters deeply— that the people doing the work are best positioned to make suggestions about how to improve the work.

We will see how this principle played out when working with an Asian company that was one of the world's largest producers of pulp and paper, as well as across industries, from manufacturing to healthcare, from technology to property management.

Adopting this proactive approach means focusing on quality, delivery, and service—and not on cutting costs. Trust that the best way to secure superior outcomes—including profits—is to gain mastery over the way you achieve them.

This book also shares a fundamental discovery about the way to create value: prioritize learning as the fundamental source of continuous improvement. All of our methods and practices are designed to generate *operational* learning—lessons and improvements derived from disciplined approaches to uncovering and resolving performance gaps. Beyond the tangible gains realized by the power of our approach, the most dynamic advantages accrue from our ever-growing capabilities.

This allows us to appreciate the compounding power of improvement. When practiced faithfully, the individual components of value boost each other in a mutually reinforcing dynamic. Producing products as needed and in flow surfaces defects quicker and increases the pressure to resolve problems immediately, at the source, which over time builds the problem-solving capability of team members. We will see how this played out at a family-owned company that makes basement doors and roof hatches.

Doing this work patiently and diligently reveals yet another key principle uniting all these ideas: that perfecting your processes is the key to superior growth. The most dramatic improvements are made from a rigorous, clear-eyed scrutiny of the actual work being done—not a disembodied discussion of it, nor an elaborate PowerPoint presentation. Enduring success results from a strong conviction in improving from the inside out. Benefits result from delivering superior value consistently, and not from seeking monopolies, holding customers captive, nor recklessly tinkering with financial engineering. The key to vitality stems from simply learning to deliver more value—and to do so by always being present at the workplace, respecting the people, and deeply understanding the work being done.

And finally, we will see how this comprehensive system for creating value works *everywhere.* Such an approach has paid off for us consistently in countless industries across the world. You do not have to follow the precise paths that we have taken to create value. But if you do create—and follow—a systematic approach to creating value that respects the people and the work being done, you will enjoy remarkable benefits that compound over time.

Creating Value will present a wide range of rich, granular company stories that illustrate the lessons vividly, tapping individual stories in a format that highlights the lessons. This book shares how relentlessly improving quality, delivery, service, and cost structure at a producer of material handling products created benefits whose gains compounded exponentially. It reveals how developing a complete system of removing waste and ensuring quality at a wiring device manufacturer required humble management and constant vigilance. How work at an electrical construction materials producer was fostered by respecting and listening to the frontline workers. And how a turnaround at a producer of industrial HVAC equipment demonstrated the value of creating quality in real time, when goods were made rather than by inspection long afterward. The book shares details from many other turnarounds and organization transformations, including a leading mattress retailer, a multinational insurance company, a property management organization, a pulp and paper maker, and a small regional hospital. This diverse selection helps codify the common principles that apply to any organization.

Let's start by going into the components of the business system in detail.

Chapter 2

Tapping the Power of a Holistic Business System

Bend at the waist, reach into a wheeled basket, scoop a large bundle of soiled restaurant napkins and bar rags, and stuff into a very large commercial washing machine. That is what our workshop team observed and smelled. To make matters worse, the worker did not have any protective apparel.

We were at a company that provided linen rental and commercial laundry services for restaurants, hotels, and spas in the South. New owners were eager to improve the quality of services and the work environment. Think hot, congested, and a smell in the air you would expect from tens of thousands of pounds of linens from yesterday's bar and restaurant scene.

The new owners had engaged me to facilitate the workshop and assist with designing their own improvement business system. The team consisted of loaders who handled the linens, a supervisor, the plant manager, and a process engineer.

The first morning, the team witnessed a few cycles of the washing machine being loaded. This was followed by listing all the problems with the process and brainstorming ideas for improvement. Scooping dirty laundry by hand was at the top of the list. One idea from the loaders was to use large bags with a drawstring on the bottom to hang the dirty laundry over the washer and release it into the washer with a pull of a string. We sent the engineer to the hardware store to buy a wheeled lifting device. On the second day we tried the new method and, while it was not perfect, the loaders no longer had to bend into the basket and scoop laundry, and the time to load was reduced by 80 percent: value created for employees, customers, and owners.

We watched the work, listened to the workers, identified the problem, tried something, standardized, and trained in the new way. One of the loaders, who spoke only Haitian Creole, gave me something sweet from his lunch. A simple application of this business system was life-changing for him. Let's define the system.

A HOLISTIC BUSINESS SYSTEM

This holistic business system is about developing people. It's about observing, listening, and making improvements (Figure 2.1). It's about eliminating waste to optimize quality,

Figure 2.1 Observe, listen, improve.

delivery, service, and cost structure. The system is hands-on by the people who do the work with a bias for action. It is not a cost-reduction project, although process improvement may result in cost reduction. It is about having the best possible quality, delivery, and service to create value for employees, customers, stakeholders, and society. It is applicable to any industry or organization. I have been involved with many transformations, and I have never seen breakthrough transformation and real value creation without utilizing the entire system.

During my consulting years, many organizations approached Moffitt Consultants with the complaint that they had been doing Lean on their own and it was not working. I would reply by asking to see their strategy deployment and their value stream analysis with improvement plans; their report-outs from continuous improvement events and event tracking; and their management systems (standard work everywhere, visual management, leader standard work). Their typical reply was we don't have all that, but we did a few workshop events. No need to criticize. Our questions alone made them realize that breakthrough improvement required a system and a rigorous commitment to executing it, not just a few events.

This business system is the result of my lifelong journey with organization transformations and continuous improvement. Its implementation has resulted in billions of dollars of value creation for employees, customers, stakeholders, and society. We have used a version of this system along with Moffitt, a business transformation consultancy, at over 100 companies.

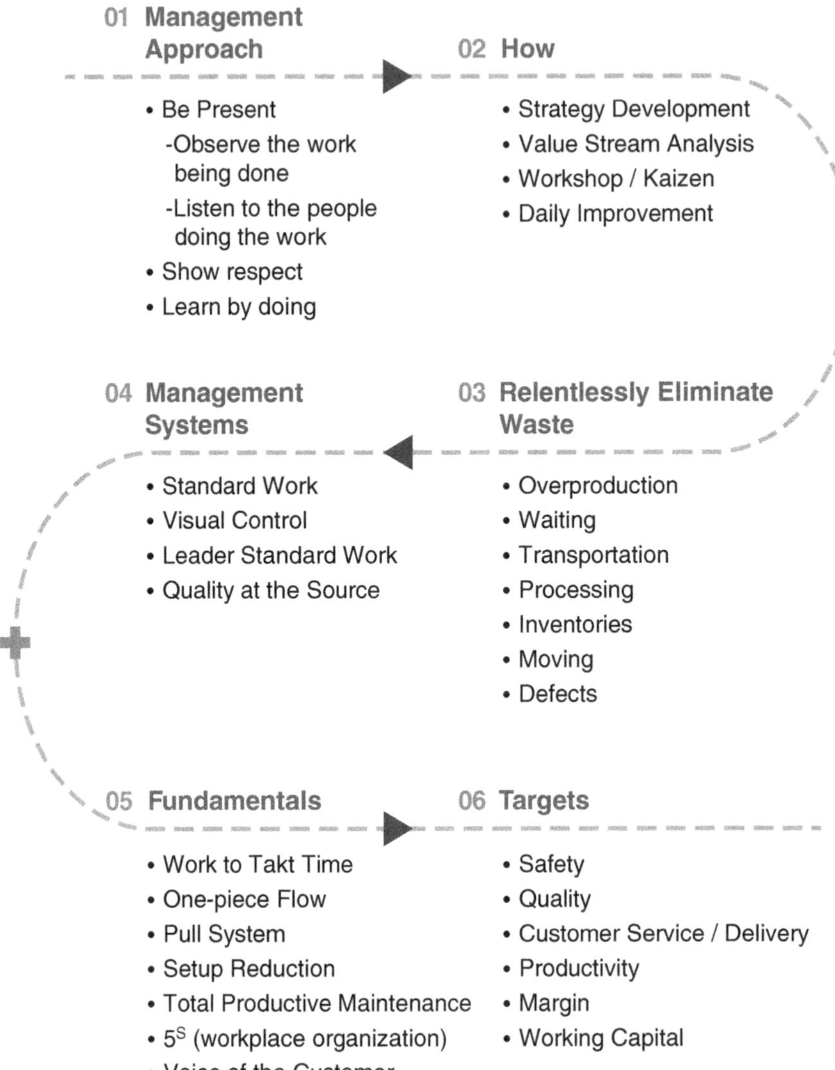

Figure 2.2 Creating Value Way.

As an essential first step, this approach must be seen as a complete and integrated business *system*. The individual components all reinforce one another; simply adopting one without simultaneously taking up all the others may lead to some improvement but rarely becomes a dynamic, steadily improving cultural approach.

This business system embodies a holistic management approach focused on continuous improvement and operational excellence. It strategically targets waste reduction through value stream analysis, daily improvement efforts, and workshop teams. It implements fundamental principles while ensuring workplace organization and accountability and sets clear targets, driving the organization toward sustained improvement and success.

Figure 2.2 illustrates key features of this holistic business system, the Creating Value Way.

MANAGEMENT APPROACH

Creating value starts with a management approach defined as *being present, observing the work being done, and listening to the people doing the work*. This is the heart of the business system and greatest contributor to value creation. This approach also applies to life, relationships, marriages, friends, and the like. If there is a common theme to every workshop described in this book or among the many workshops I have participated in over the last 30 years, this is it: Be present, observe the work being done, and listen to those doing the work.

HOW(S)

The starting point for a comprehensive approach to creating value is strategy deployment—a fully articulated vision of the direction an organization is going. Creating a clear and inclusive plan ensures that an organization's strategic goals drive progress at every level, aligning the entire organization toward key objectives. Once there is a direction, value stream analysis provides a roadmap and workshops get you there.

Companies that have been successful have found that working with a mentor or teacher is crucial to getting started with this process. It's difficult to learn just from a book, and somebody who has experience with this, who has been through many implementations, can really accelerate the implementation and improve success.

It helps to commit 1 to 2 percent of your employment to continuous improvement. So, if you have 500 employees, you might have 5 to 10 people working full-time on continuous improvement. Typically, these are people from all different levels of the organization. They participate in workshops and are trained so that they can lead workshops on their own to facilitate continuous improvement in the organization. Most importantly, they focus on people development.

In many cases, companies can free up people through the implementation of this business system, which happens as they eliminate waste in the value stream. These people can be deployed to the improvement office. Having people working full-time on implementing their business system results in a very high return.

One of the most vital ways to open people's minds is for the executive to participate in a workshop at another organization. When somebody participates at another company's workshop, it must be the senior leader. No "sending all our engineers to learn at this other company that's doing a great job with continuous improvement." That could happen down the road, but this is not something that's delegated. It's got to be led from the top by senior executives who have seen it in action and really understand the process and opened their minds.

For me, that was Wiremold. I was sales manager at Crouse-Hinds, and Wiremold was our number one customer. Art Byrne invited me to participate in a workshop at Wiremold, and that's what really opened my mind to this whole process. I got to witness the work firsthand and talk to the people doing the work and participate in the workshops and benefit from it. It was energizing and opened this executive's mind. I also realized we needed to have alignment throughout our company regarding improvement activities. Enter strategy deployment.

STRATEGY DEPLOYMENT

The power of strategy deployment lies in its ability to create organizational coherence by connecting strategic planning with tactical execution, transforming abstract objectives into concrete actions while preventing the common disconnect between leadership aspirations and frontline activities.

Strategy deployment promotes deep thinking and collaboration. Typically, the first-year and third-year objectives, or "What," are suggested at the executive level. The next level in the organization suggests strategic initiatives or "How(s)" and targets to improve or "Key Results." Back and forth discussion is the key to the process. Targets are expected to be breakthrough. The corners show the linkages.

Figure 2.3 shows a great example of a practical format to adopt when it comes to deploying strategy.

When you get started with strategy deployment, keep in mind that it takes two to three years to get good at. That entails two to three cycles—not something that you are an expert at the first time you go through. Mastery takes multiple years of practice.

The first time could start off with a workshop that includes the executive team and the people who report to the executive team. If you had five plant managers, they would all participate. Include the CEO, president, CFO, and head of HR. Hold a day of training orientation sharing examples from other organizations. This represents a powerful way of learning because, unlike book learning or PowerPoint slides, seeing real examples from other organizations really fixes the key learning points in people's minds.

Proceed by brainstorming on the objectives. What are the one-year objectives and three-year objectives? Typically, that's done by the executive team. Then the targets to improve are set by the next level down. That's done through catchball between the two levels.

Catchball involves a back-and-forth exchange of ideas, feedback, and responsibilities between different organizational levels, like tossing a ball between participants. Starting with broad strategic goals from leadership, each level refines these objectives and implementation plans before passing them along. This iterative communication ensures strategic alignment, builds consensus, creates shared ownership, and helps transform high-level strategies into actionable plans with organization-wide buy-in. Catchball contrasts with traditional top-down approaches by emphasizing two-way dialogue that makes strategies both realistic and widely accepted.

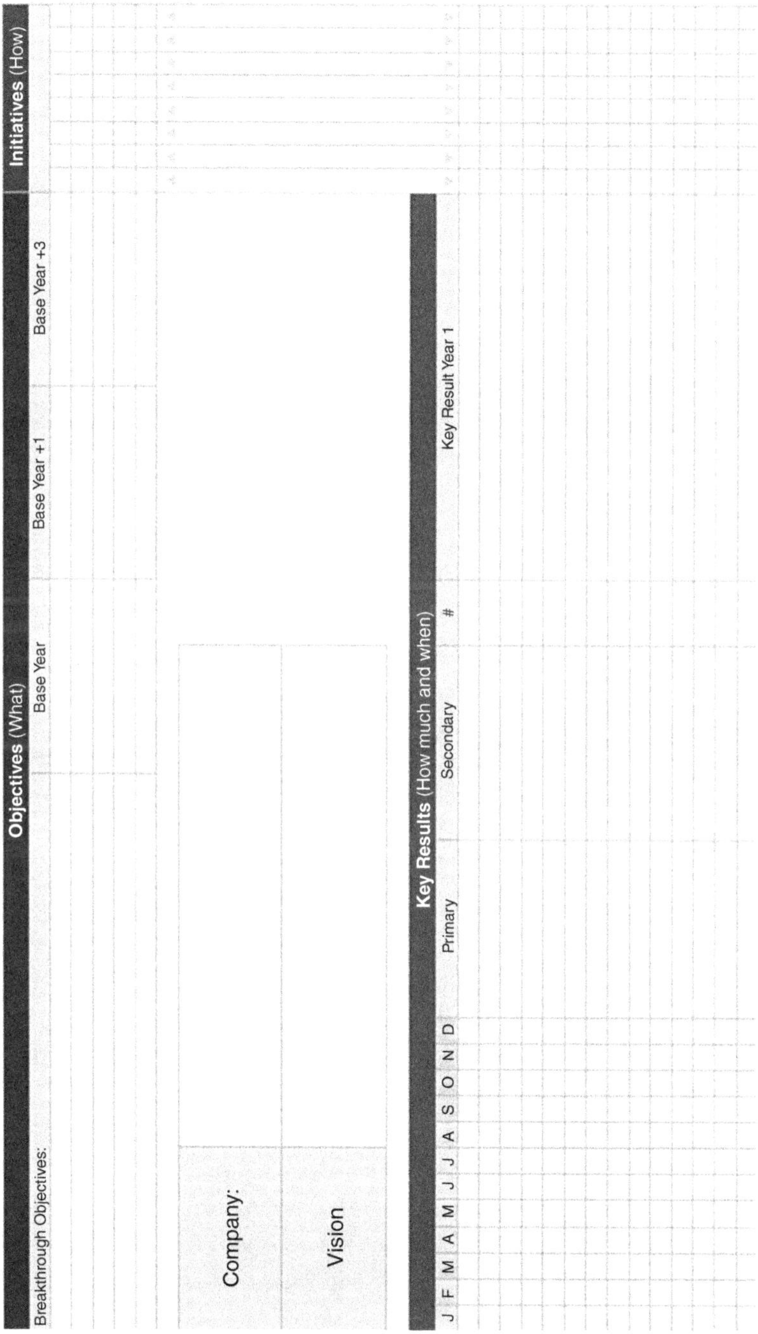

Initiatives (How)

Objectives (What)

Breakthrough Objectives:

Base Year

Base Year +1

Base Year +3

Company:

Vision

Key Results (How much and when)

Primary

Secondary

#

Key Result Year 1

J F M A M J J A S O N D

Figure 2.3 Strategy deployment X-matrix.

For the first time through, we've got everybody in the room. We ask in a broad sense: What should our one-year objectives be? We explain what we mean by *breakthrough* objectives. These are not modest or minor objectives that you establish so that everybody is ensured of making their bonuses. These are ambitious stretch goals that set the bar high. If you set the bar high enough, you have a much better chance of achieving something meaningful, as opposed to setting the bar lower, which means that once you get close to it, you'll probably stop.

We don't want to stop. We want to stretch. Not fully realizing the breakthrough objectives doesn't mean failure. We might in fact get 20–30 or even 50 percent improvement in any particular area. The goal might be 50 percent improvement, and we might get to 40 percent. That doesn't mean we failed. In fact, that ends up being kind of awesome: Wow, we got 40 percent improvement.

We ask this team to establish the objectives for the next year. Then we say: What are the objectives going to be three years out? Because we want to be thinking about a plan to achieve this year's objectives, but to what end?

We went through this process at a national mattress retailer. At the time they had a few hundred locations. They set a three-year objective for many times that number of stores. Everybody looked at that number every month and thought, wow, we've got to get going on that right now if we're going to be there in three years. It's important to simply get the brainstorming process going for how you are going to get there. The process of getting the team there is critical. That national mattress retailer that started their journey with a version of this business system now has thousands of locations and was recently acquired for $5 billion.

On a monthly basis, we're looking at the strategy deployment X-matrix, which every month shows the targets to improve. The ones that are making it are green—great. We don't talk about those. We focus on the ones that are in red, and work as a team to get them to green.

When these targets are in red, we're not telling people anything. We're not bossing them around. We're supporting them. We're asking this question: What do we need to get to green? The question might come up in a monthly review where we've got plant managers and HR and engineering. The issue might emerge that you simply need more resources from engineering or some other form of help. You may have to add resources, or you make other adjustments, but the focus is squarely on what to do to change course and converge on green. The focus is decidedly not, "Gee, we're red, we're not working, we're behind. We're not doing a good job. We're got to crack the whip." The focus is deliberately asking: How do we get to green?

This becomes a focused way of framing problems in an achievable way. It's very forward-looking, and it's laser-focused on removing every kind and type of blame, or wasteful reflection about what we did wrong.

In other words, throughout this whole business system, we focus on the process, and not on the people, not on blame. This is not about blaming people for processes getting out of whack, which they do for all kinds of reasons. We just focus on process and need to get to the root cause in order to solve these types of challenges.

Focusing on process means diligently digging into problems and establishing pure causality about why they occur—finding the true root cause of defects. There are many different ways to distill a problem to a root cause. Fishbone, for example, is a popular method for determining root cause, for teasing out the source of waste.

Asking five whys is another way of discovering root cause. That's where you keep asking "why" until you get to the point where the workshop team realizes that if they fix this isolated challenge, that will solve the problem at the source— the point where resolving it prevents it permanently from recurring.

Imagine that there's a puddle of water on the floor where somebody slipped and was injured. When we investigated, we asked, "How did that happen?" The quick conclusion was that maintenance was not doing their job. They should be cleaning the floors every day. Or else that there should be a drain in the floor that naturally deals with puddles.

What we really needed to ask is "Why is there water on the floor?" Maybe it wasn't a spill out of the machine or a function of someone doing their work. Maybe it was a leak in the roof, meaning that it wasn't a problem from a machine or spillage.

If there was a leak in the roof, then the question is why is it there? Maybe because we haven't done maintenance on our roof in years—and if so, why not? Could it be that we don't have a plan for ongoing maintenance for roof repair? If so, the short-term resolution is, well, let's fix it, but the proper long-term plan is to ensure that we have a plan to keep that roof in proper repair so we don't have leaks again. That guarantees that we don't have spillage again, and we don't have a safety incident. The way to know that you have reached the right level of "why" is when you get to the point where this particular issue gets resolved so that the problem won't recur. You just keep asking questions until you get to that point. You continue to drill down until there is no next level. You keep asking questions until you've hit the true root cause.

Following these principles gradually eliminates wasteful blame and focuses on the process of productive shared problem-solving. We observe, listen, and improve together. If it's the leak on the factory floor, we're not going to solve that in an office. You go to the factory, and you look up and you see it's coming from there. Asking why is part of that listening process. Observe, listen, improve. Everything relates back to this process. You stick to this approach even when it feels counterintuitive because the natural inclination would be to blame people, because traditional management finds fault and assigns blame.

In fact, we coach people not to use the word "you." Framing questions impersonally represents a powerful way of removing blame from an analysis of the situation. As soon as you say, "Why did *you* only get through 45 pieces last hour; the goal is 60," then what that person hears is that they are being attacked, and they go into defensive mode. The way we should ask that question is: "Why were only 45 units produced?" Now we're focusing on the process, not the person. That creates an opportunity for someone to reply, "The air gun didn't work," or cite other issues. When you're focused on the process, not the person, you're setting up the problem in a solvable way. It's a small approach that makes a big difference and gets out of the blame game. When that chart says only 45, we can then focus on what in the process keeps us from getting to the standard of 60.

This ties through the whole system. We have strategy deployment, value stream analysis, workshops, and management systems. It's a focus on the process. We see these problems as close to real time as possible and can help with solutions. This is a system of running toward problems.

Strategy deployment cascades throughout an organization and results are updated frequently (Figure 2.4). If a target is on-track, it is coded green, and if it is off-track, it's red.

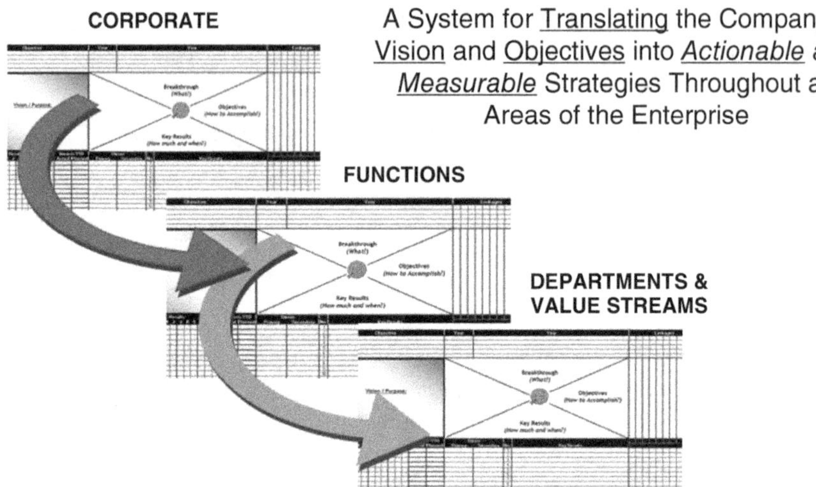

Figure 2.4   Cascading objectives and goals.

I have run entire businesses with this one-page document. On a site visit or in a monthly business review, I can learn in seconds the priorities and if they are on- or off-track. We focus then on what was red or off-track. Everyone is collaborating on what is needed to "get to green." If most of the targets are achieved, we are confident we could achieve the top objectives.

One of the hardest parts about strategy deployment is what we call deselecting: when you've got multiple objectives and boil it down to the critical breakthrough few. Typically, when we brainstorm the key results or targets to improve, the bottom section of the X-matrix, you probably end up with way too many targets to improve. And they are all important, right?

Well, no, wrong. Any time that happens is a clear failure point. Squeezing 50 or 100 targets in there prevents you from staying focused on hitting them, reviewing them, or realizing them in a granular way. You need to take all but the critical few off the plate and focus on what is most important.

We discovered this at a manufacturer of HVAC equipment when I was serving in an executive role. We were working with a coach and presented a list of 40 or 50 things that we believed we needed to get done over the course of the year. And the coach said, "You know that's not achievable, right? Do you live in a world where every time something comes up, you just add it to the list of what's got to get done now?"

This challenged us to admit that we were feeling overwhelmed—that adding even more items to the list just increased this feeling of having too much to do, not to mention that we were simply doing a mediocre job as a result. The organization was experiencing pervasive frustration, and folks didn't really know where they needed to focus their time and effort. Strategy deployment is all about focusing your time and effort. When you have 50 or 75 targets to improve, it's just not possible to focus an organization. Finally, we boiled it down to under 20. It worked because we got focused on the critical few.

Our strategy deployment cascaded down from our corporate headquarters to each of our multiple factories, which linked together and cascaded the strategy—the objectives and targets to improve. All the way down to the production line, people knew how what they were working on tied into the objectives at the high level. It really worked for us because we got focused. Of course, we made sure that we got every item done.

How did we choose the critical few? We start off by defining *value*. Companies often mistakenly focus on cost. Instead, consider what's important to the people who do the work, to the customers, and to the owners. We evaluate based on what impact they're going to have on value to them. We reduce the number of goals by asking what the employee, the customer, and the owner values in the process, what is important to them.

As for who participates in this process of setting priorities, you want to include stakeholders from as many different functions and different levels within the organization as possible. You don't want all C-suite people—nor do you want all people who do the work. You're trying to put a workshop team together and cover all those bases. You might not have the vice president of HR on the team, but someone who works as an associate in HR in the factory. You could have somebody who actually does the work, and a supervisor. You might have someone from finance, either the CFO or an accountant. What you're trying to do is cover all the functions in a diversified way—not all C-suite nor all entry level.

Team composition is important. If you don't have the right people in the room representing not only the different functions but the different layers of the organization, you will fail. Having the right people in the room getting buy-in is essential. It makes a clear statement that this is the new way of doing things.

Strategy deployment is not merely a planning exercise, but a transformative approach to organizational alignment that connects strategic vision with frontline execution. Its power lies in creating coherence throughout an organization by translating high-level objectives into concrete, measurable actions that every team member can understand and contribute to. The journey of successful strategy deployment requires patience and persistence. As we've seen, mastery typically takes two to three years of practice through multiple cycles. Organizations must embrace this learning curve, recognizing that the first implementation will not be perfect but serves as an essential foundation for future refinement.

Successful strategy deployment hinges on several key principles. Organizations must focus on the critical few targets rather than attempting to pursue too many simultaneously, ruthlessly prioritizing to maintain focus. By concentrating on processes rather than people, strategy deployment fosters a culture of continuous improvement and problem-solving rather than finger-pointing. The catchball process between organizational levels ensures collaborative problem-solving with two-way communication, better solutions, and stronger buy-in from all stakeholders. Setting ambitious stretch goals or breakthrough objectives, rather than easily attainable targets, drives meaningful improvement even when the objectives aren't fully realized. Visual management through the X-matrix and color-coded tracking systems creates transparency and focuses attention on areas needing support. Diligent root cause analysis prevents recurrence of problems by addressing their true source and systemic issues. Finally, involving diverse stakeholders from various functions and levels ensures inclusive participation with comprehensive perspectives and organizational alignment.

When implemented effectively, strategy deployment becomes more than a management tool—it evolves into an organizational operating system that aligns daily activities with long-term vision. It creates clarity, focus, and a shared sense of purpose that propels the organization toward breakthrough performance. The true measure of successful strategy deployment isn't perfection in execution, but rather the organization's enhanced ability to identify challenges early, solve problems collaboratively, and continuously adapt while maintaining alignment with its strategic objectives. This dynamic capability becomes increasingly valuable in today's rapidly changing business environment, where agility and coherence must coexist for sustainable success.

FROM WHERE WE ARE GOING, TO HOW WE ARE GOING TO GET THERE

If strategy deployment shows us where we are going, value stream analysis and improvement planning (VSA/IP) is the roadmap of how we are going to get there (Figure 2.5). This is a structured approach to map, analyze, and improve the flow of value through an organization's processes. It focuses on identifying work that adds value to the customer and eliminating what does not.

The process starts with a team defining what the customer values. This is important because it guides the team when analyzing current conditions and creating the improvement plan. The team then observes the process. If it's a factory, we walk and observe the entire production process, starting

Value Stream Analysis in 9 Steps

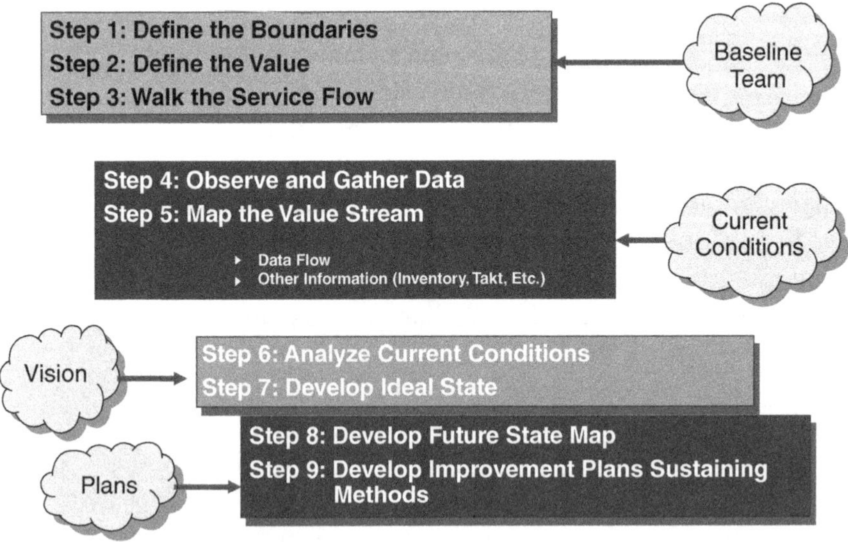

Figure 2.5   Value stream analysis steps.

with the finished product and moving upstream. This helps us understand the flow and what triggers movement of material. For an administrative process, observation may be at the computer.

The workshop team documents the process from when a customer wants a product or service to getting paid by that customer. The map is at a high level (Figure 2.6). The purpose is not to create a perfect rendition but to be able to see where the gaps are in providing value for the customer. The map also shows the flow of information and material and all the waiting time between tasks.

Once the workshop team has documented the current condition, they brainstorm what would be the ideal state and what it would take to get there. While we rarely achieve the ideal state, I am not surprised how close the team usually comes with a plan.

Not only does the value stream analysis provide a roadmap, but the process of creating it helps achieve buy-in for implementation. It grounds everyone in the nitty-gritty work of actually creating value. We're going to observe the real work carefully and without any misconceptions or biases.

This was borne out at my work at an equipment manufacturer of medical implants such as replacement knees, hips, and shoulders. I was facilitating the work, and we started by walking the process by which they made a knee. This was an elaborate process! It stretched from one building to another building to another building and back.

The location was in the Deep South, and when we walked the value stream it was pouring rain. One of the higher-ups

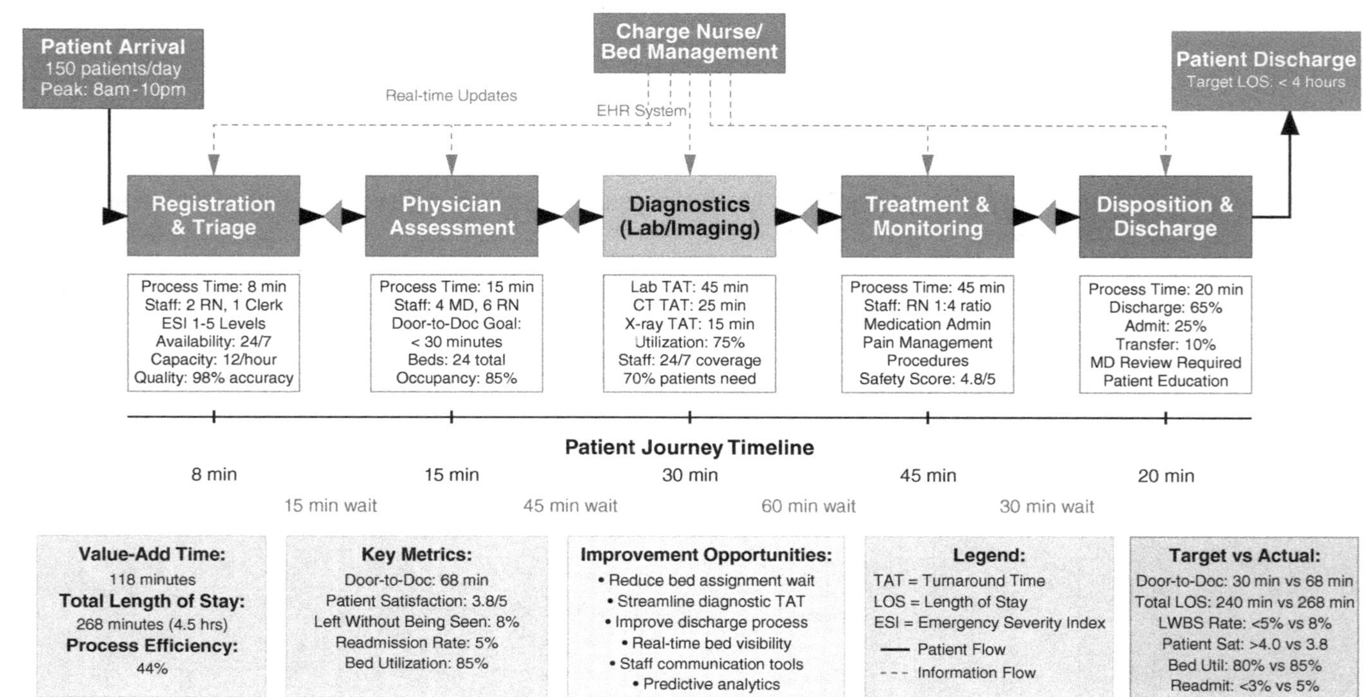

Figure 2.6   Value stream map example.

on the team said, "Well, we know what goes on in that other building, so we don't have to go there, right?" He didn't want to get wet. He wanted to retreat to the conference room and map from memory and computer printouts. I responded, "No, if the parts have to do it, we have to do it." There simply is no substitute for going to the workplace and observing the work being done.

We walked in the pouring rain to that next building, and then to the next building, and then back. We walked over a mile to observe how they made a simple part. It took all day, and the obvious takeaway from this mile-long walk was that if we put all these various processes in the same room, we could take that flow down from a mile to hundreds of yards.

We discovered that the real problem wasn't that we needed a new piece of equipment or that we had this big bottleneck (which, to be fair, is something that you often see). The problem was simply a result of how the business had grown to produce the product. It had terrible flow that had worsened over time. It took all day, and we discovered that the component traveled 1.26 miles, had 38 moves, and entailed 25 storage locations. The actual work time was 8 hours, and total time was 85 days. That's a lot of sleeping parts. People were in fact shocked to discover that they were working on the part less than 1 percent of the time! It is not unusual when a value stream is mapped for the first time to discover that the actual time making the product is less than 5 percent of the total time.

The leader update meeting at the end of the first day was humbling for everyone and at the same time motivating. Everyone internalized the value stream and had a sense of urgency to improve the flow and therefore improve customer service and productivity.

The improvement plan, without any major investment, was to reduce the days to produce by 81 percent and travel distance by 36 percent. They recognized that there were still additional improvements to be made, but this was achievable in the short term.

We needed—and got—buy-in from the entire team about an appropriate improvement plan. All of this started with a simple walk observing the process.

Value stream analysis and improvement planning (VSA/IP) serves as the critical bridge between strategic goals and tactical implementation. This structured approach provides organizations with both a clear picture of current reality and a practical roadmap for meaningful improvement. The case study of the medical equipment manufacturer powerfully illustrates several key principles. Direct observation is nonnegotiable—despite resistance and physical discomfort, walking the entire process revealed insights that would have remained hidden in conference room discussions or computer printouts. The discovery that parts traveled 1.26 miles through 38 moves and 25 storage locations could only come from firsthand observation.

The gap between work time and total time is often shocking. Finding that actual value-adding work constituted less than 1 percent of the total production time (8 hours of work spread across 85 days) created both humility and motivation. This revelation is common when organizations first map their value streams, with value-adding time typically below 5 percent. Significant improvements often require minimal investment.

The team developed a plan to reduce production time by 81 percent and travel distance by 36 percent without major capital expenditures. The waste was hiding in plain sight within the process flow that had evolved haphazardly over time. The mapping process itself builds consensus and commitment. By experiencing the process together and collectively uncovering its flaws, the team developed shared understanding and a sense of urgency for improvement. This collaborative approach ensured everyone was aligned with both the problems and the solutions. Value stream analysis transforms abstract strategic objectives into concrete, actionable plans grounded in the reality of how work actually happens. By revealing the enormous gap between current and ideal states, it creates both the roadmap and the motivation needed to drive meaningful change. Most importantly, it shifts the focus from departmental or functional silos to the end-to-end flow of value to customers—the ultimate purpose of any organization.

WORKSHOP (ALSO CALLED KAIZEN)

Another "how" in the business model are workshops. These can be seen as the journey to eliminate waste. In the context of the business model, a workshop brings together a team, including the people who do the work, which meets for 3–5 days with a bias for action now. A 50 percent improvement done today is better than wishful perfection someday. The team observes the current state, asks why, identifies waste, determines root cause, tries countermeasures, reflects, and creates a sustainability plan with standard work and visual management. The ethos is "do it now." Dozens of workshops are profiled in this book and followed this process (Figure 2.7).

Then there's daily improvement, where a culture of continuous improvement leads people to look at the work and continuously make improvements. Cultural change is neither

Figure 2.7   Improvement process.

purely top-down nor bottom-up. This practice is a collaborative effort where leadership provides vision and support, and employees take ownership of improvements. Successful transformations occur when the two approaches are aligned and mutually reinforcing. This may take many years.

This chapter presents a holistic business system, which focuses on developing people through continuous improvement. The system is guided by three key components: a management approach of being present, observing work, and listening to workers; strategic methods including strategy deployment (using X-matrixes to set breakthrough objectives), value stream analysis (mapping processes to identify waste), and improvement workshops. Rather than being a cost-cutting initiative, this system aims to create value for employees, customers, stakeholders, and society by optimizing quality, delivery, and service. All components must work together as an integrated system, with leadership involvement being critical for success.

Chapter 3

Sustaining the Dynamic Power of a Holistic Business System

"Why are you rust-proofing a stainless-steel part?" asked a team member. The workshop team was focused on improving the manufacturing of a part. We were working on a simple product called a breather drain, which is a one-way stainless-steel valve that helps condensation come out of an enclosure where moisture is building up.

Initially, it took months to make this simple part, and each part traveled over a mile during the manufacturing process.

It went through multiple machining areas, a wash process, passivation, assembly, and packaging before being stored in the warehouse. Although a significant amount of inventory had been built based on forecasted need, the sizes the customers needed weren't always available. On-time delivery was accomplished only 50 percent of the time.

We examined the current state and all the steps in the manufacturing process. In one of the steps, the part was sent out to a third party to be passivated (a process that prevents rust). Because this stainless-steel part was already fully rust-resistant, the passivation process was both unnecessary and redundant. A member of the workshop team, an accountant we'll call Fresh Eyes, knew nothing about the manufacturing process. As he listened to the steps in the process, he asked why we were overprocessing.

Fresh Eyes:	Why are we rust-proofing stainless steel, which does not rust?
Engineer:	It's in the specifications.
Fresh Eyes:	Why is it in the spec?
Engineer:	The customer requires it.
Fresh Eyes:	Why would the customer require it?
Engineer:	Customer says it is rusting.
Fresh Eyes:	Why do you think it's rusting?
Engineer:	There is probably residual material on the part from the tool used to cut the metal.
The solution was simple:	Wash all the rust-prone tooling residual off the part.

In addition to eliminating unnecessary work, the team improved flow by moving all the scattered equipment into a cell during the workshop. They added a used household dishwasher to clean the part. A long, expensive process was replaced by—quite literally—a secondhand Maytag.

The parts no longer had to move between departments or outside the factory, reducing wastes from transportation, unnecessary processing, waiting, and eliminating finished goods inventory.

The operator would make parts today for the orders that came in yesterday. Parts were produced to takt time, using one-piece flow based on pull from the customer. (Takt time refers to the time for product assembly that is needed to meet customer demand.)

The focus on eliminating waste in this area resulted in lead times being reduced from months to one day, improving customer service and increasing on-time delivery to 100 percent. Productivity increased by over 80 percent. The working capital impact was in the hundreds of thousands of dollars.

RELENTLESSLY ELIMINATE WASTE

Each of the wastes listed in the business system represents opportunities for improvement. They are a critical focus because eliminating waste is essential to maximizing value or providing what's important to employees, customers, and owners. Remember, a key attribute of this business system is to eliminate waste by observing, listening, and making improvements.

These are the basic forms of waste (from business system model in Chapter 2, Figure 2.2):

- Overproduction: Anytime we produce in advance of when needed or in too great a quantity, we may cause something that is needed now by the customer to be delayed.

- Waiting: An employee waiting for work, the work waiting for an employee, or the customer waiting.
- Transportation: How far or how often we move products or information.
- Processing: Work that may no longer be necessary.
- Inventories: Inventory is always waste. If a company could receive material, parts, and information just in time, it would not need large inventories. If there is not good flow or JIT, the question becomes what ideal amount is needed.
- Moving: How far an employee needs to move or reach.
- Defects: Anytime we must redo work is bad, and any time a defect or quality issue gets to a customer is tragic.

FUNDAMENTALS (FROM BUSINESS SYSTEM MODEL IN CHAPTER 2, FIGURE 2.2)

Traditionally, when someone buys a men's suit, a tailor recuts and sews to get the suit to fit. Because it was not made to fit the customer, this is overprocessing—a defect. At a manufacturer of men's suits, the lead time to make a suit was approximately eight weeks and the cycle time or touch time (someone cutting or sewing) was around three hours. This is a typical ratio between lead time and touch time when a team does the initial value stream analysis. The long lead time was the result of producing parts of the suit in very large batches and storing the suit components in a warehouse until it was time to assemble, also in batches. The quality of the suit is never as good when it is recut and sewed as it is when making it right the first time.

The challenge was this: How could a large manufacturer with long lead times provide what the customer wanted, making the suit right the first time, and fast? The solution was to create a process for the customer to go into a department store and have their measurements taken and sent to the factory. The factory would make the suit in one-piece flow and deliver it to the department store in seven days for the customer to pick up. Make it right the first time and no rework of cutting and sewing.

Many workshops were held to reduce lead times and produce a suit to order in seven days. For example, the current state to make a sleeve required large batches moving between departments. A team moved eight operations to produce a sleeve into one area called a cell. Time observations were made, and the work was balanced between each operation, so each operator had a takt time of work. A sleeve came off the end of the line every 43 seconds. Many similar cells were created and linked together so a suit could be made to order in a few days.

After many years this producer of men's suits continues to flourish. Although there were significant gains in productivity, it is the improved delivery and quality, not labor costs, that are the drivers of their success. Beyond this company, US garment production is making a comeback because of gains in quality, delivery, and productivity across the industry. Let's explain a few of the fundamentals utilized by this company and many of the workshops in this book:

- **Work to Takt Time:** The rate at which products need to be produced to meet customer demand without overproduction or delays. It is calculated by dividing available production time by the number of units the customer requires within the same time frame. Example calculation:
  - Available Production Time: 7.5 hours per day (450 minutes)
  - Customer Demand: 225 units per day

  Takt Time = 450 minutes/225 units = 2 minutes per unit

This means that one unit must be completed every two minutes to meet customer demand. In order to meet customer demand, the time to produce should match or be slightly less than takt time. This also applies to office tasks.

- **One-piece flow:** Processing material or information one at a time rather than in batches. The benefits are faster delivery, reduced inventory, and improved quality management.
- **Pull:** Only produce what product or service is needed, when it is needed, by the customer. It is not based on a forecast.
- **Setup reduction:** Minimizing the time it takes to switch from providing one product or service to another. Benefits include reduced lead times and increased flexibility. It's often a contributor to establishing "pull."
- **Total productive maintenance:** Involves everyone to improve overall equipment effectiveness. Operators provide autonomous maintenance activities such as cleaning, inspection, and lubrication. Maintenance personnel provide preventive and predictive maintenance tasks.
- **5S's (workplace organization).** Methodology is used to create a safe and efficient work environment.
    - **Sort** involves getting rid of everything that is not needed in an area.
    - **Set in order** organizes everything in designated locations.
    - **Shine** keeps the area clean.
    - **Standardization** involves clear standards for maintaining the first three S's.
    - **Sustain** refers to activities such as audits to continually improve the area.

- **Voice of the customer.** Translating unfiltered customer needs and expectations into specific product or service requirements. The voice of the customer process drives innovation by creating a systematic approach to understanding customer needs, challenges, and expectations. By collecting, analyzing, and acting on customer feedback through surveys, interviews, focus groups, and data analytics, organizations identify unmet needs and pain points that would otherwise remain invisible. This customer intelligence provides clear direction for innovation efforts, reducing development risks and increasing the likelihood of market success. It also breaks internal biases by introducing external perspectives that challenge assumptions, while establishing feedback loops that enable continuous improvement and refinement of offerings. Companies that excel at implementing create cultures where innovation is naturally directed toward solving real problems rather than pursuing technology for its own sake, resulting in more valuable and differentiated products and services.

MANAGEMENT SYSTEMS

I supported an insurance company on their process improvement journey. While facilitating many workshops for this company, I saw how management systems were crucial to organization transformation and could create hundreds of millions of dollars in value and change a culture at a non-manufacturing company.

One workshop was focused on how a claim was received. In the current state, the policyholder would call to make a claim. The call would be received by a call center that would take the basic information. That information would be transferred to the agent who was responsible for resolving that claim. Typically, the claim agent would have to call the policyholder to get additional information. Phone tag was common. This could result in days of waiting. Anytime work is handed off, waste is introduced into the system.

The countermeasure was to set up a system where the call could go directly to an available claim agent. This eliminated both the call center and the handoff. When the policyholder called, they were speaking with the person who would handle the claim. The policyholder did not have to repeat information on multiple calls with multiple people. The claim agent was able to get most, if not all, of the information they needed to proceed with the claim. In many cases, this eliminated multiple days from the claim process and reduced the wastes of waiting (caused by handoff process), defects (caused by the call center not getting all the information needed), and overprocessing (the policyholder had to explain the claim to both the call center and the claim agent). A follow-up workshop focused on increasing the number of claims that could be resolved in a single phone call—in other words, one and done.

I remember a case where a policyholder in a remote area had their side-view mirror ripped off. Traditionally, the policyholder would call the call center, the call center would pass the claim along to a claim agent, and the claim agent would then contact the customer to get more information. This usually took a few calls to accommodate when both parties were available. Next, the claim agent would send out an inspector, the inspector would send in an estimate, and the claim agent would process the claim and let the policyholder know the amount that was going to be covered. In the new approach, the call came to the claim agent, and while on the phone the policyholder sent a picture of the damage. The claim agent was then able to look up what it would cost to replace a side-view mirror and tell the policyholder that a check was going out immediately. Needless to say, the "one and done" result delighted the policyholder.

During another workshop, a new method of visual control was developed, leading to breakthrough improvement in customer service. The insurance company had learned from a workshop focused on voice of the customer that if a property claim was resolved in seven days or less, the customer would be delighted. Monthly reports showed approximately 20 percent of the claims were resolved in less than seven days. Unfortunately, learning at the end of the month that the goal was missed was too late to correct and determine causes.

The team created a whiteboard for each claim agent to be able to track in real time how claims were progressing (Figure 3.1).

When a claim agent received a claim, they would write it on a small Post-it Note and place it on the board. Each day a claim was opened, the claim agent would move it to the appropriate day and into the category of whether the

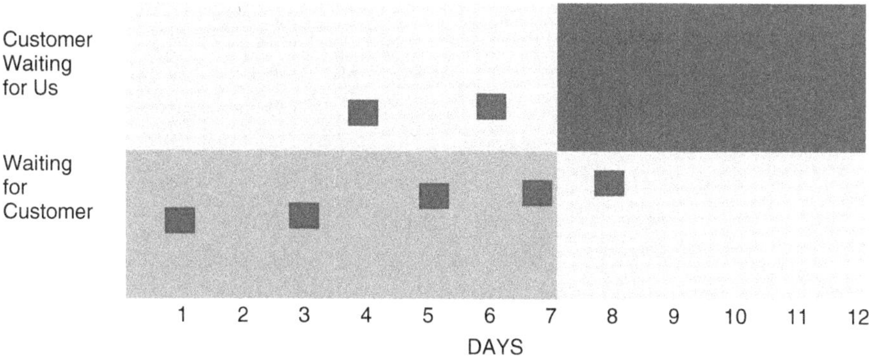

Figure 3.1   Visual management.

customer was waiting on them or if they were waiting on the customer. The manager and fellow claim agents were continually looking at the boards. If a claim ended up in red, that meant the goal was missed and the claim was more than seven days old, and the customer was waiting for the claim agent. As claims got into the six- or seven-day range, they received a lot of attention and problem-solving. The focus was not on blame but on how they could work together to make sure no one had a claim go over seven days.

They did not need to wait until the end of the month to see if they were achieving the seven-day goal. They knew because of daily visual management what the monthly report was going to be. In the end they improved claims processed under seven days from 20 percent to over 80 percent. This was an incredible example of how visual control can impact the customer. Morale also improved because everyone was working together toward the same goal and help was provided when needed.

This insurance company held many workshops focused on standard work. Each team would focus on a small part of the value stream. They would observe, listen, and improve. The improvements would be documented in standard work. As in a manufacturing environment, the standard work was time-based, actionable by the people who did the work, generated at the point of use, and reflected what was critical to quality. Nonmanufacturing processes can benefit from time-based instructions.

Most importantly, we learned that empowerment is not about trying to figure out your job every day. Empowerment is about being able to make improvements regarding your job. Standard work must be followed by everyone, every time. However, if someone has a better way, they're empowered to suggest and implement improvement. Remarkably, they had one set of standard work that was approximately 15 pages and in the first few months it had over 50 changes or improvements made to it.

Now that they had extensive standard work and visual control, they saw the urgency to make sure somebody was paying attention to that standard work, it was being followed, and problems were being resolved as close to real time as possible. For this they created leader standard work or work instructions for everyone in supervisory roles (Figure 3.2).

Like all workshops, we started with documenting reality. For prework, managers kept track of everything they did for two weeks prior. Many managers were unclear about the requirements of their job. It is common that people are promoted to supervisory and managerial positions but are never really given clear guidance or training to be successful.

The team then identified activities, which were people development, necessary, and waste. The team set a goal of 50 percent of the manager's time to be spent on people development activities:

- Is there standard work?
- Have people been trained in it?
- Does everyone have the tools and resources to be successful?
- Is it being followed?
- What do the visual controls say?
- Are employee issues and problems being resolved?

A plan was developed to eliminate the tasks the managers were performing that were categorized as waste and minimize tasks that were necessary. The outcome was the creation of leader standard work that set clear expectations on

Leader Standard Work

Manager / Supervisor to check off tasks as they are accomplished. Manager's Supervisor will verify completion once a week.

Task No.	Task	Mins	Frequency (D/W)	Location	MON	TUE	WED	THU	FRI	SAT	One Up check-off	Comments
1												
2												
3												
4												
5												
6												
7												
8												
9												
10												
11												
12												
Comments												

Figure 3.2   Leader standard work common format.

responsibilities and how time should be spent, including at least 50 percent on people development. Although difficult to quantify, many at this insurance company believed this was the single biggest contributor to the company's incredible transformation.

Another workshop focused on standard work and reducing the time to resolve a claim for property theft. Documenting the current state, the team discovered that it took an average of three weeks to settle a property theft claim. The longest part of the three weeks was waiting approximately two weeks for the police report. Then, when they finally got the police report, it would be attached to the claim.

The team asked:

- Is it used to settle the claim?
    - No

- Why?
    - It's not accurate.

- Why is it not accurate?
    - Maybe the policyholder forgot to mention something, or the police officer made a mistake writing it down.

If you're not relying on the police report to settle a claim, instead of waiting for that report, why not just go ahead and settle the claim?

The outcome was that if the police report did not come in in a timely manner, the employee could go ahead and resolve the claim using what the policyholder submitted. When the police report did come in, it was attached to the claim for filing—no different from what was happening before. The team did put in place a few exceptions for red-flag claims, such as exceptionally large dollars or an instance where the policyholder had never even called the police. The average time to resolve was reduced from three weeks to less than five days, a true value creator for the customer.

For many organizations the most challenging part of the improvement process is sustaining the improvements. Three things must be present for sustainability: standard work, visual management, and leader standard work (Figure 3.3).

Standard work: Instructions are time-based, actionable by the people who do the work, readily available for use, and reflect quality and safety. It is difficult to make any improvement if there is not a standard to improve on. Standard work is needed everywhere, even in the office. If improvements are made often, so should the standard work be updated. If I see standard work that has not been updated in the last 30 days, I conclude that no improvements have been made. This is a red flag for an ineffective business system.

Standard Work
- Time based
- Actionable
- Reflects Quality & Safety
- At point of use

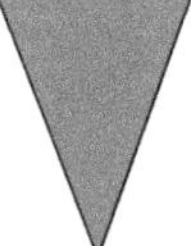

Leader Standard Work
- Asks, "Is there Standard Work?"
- "Is it being followed?"
- "Are we getting results?"
- *Real-time problem-solving*

Visual Management
- Real-time performance & problem identification
- Shows trend and goal
- Actionable
- Easy to see
- Answers, "What does good look like?"

Figure 3.3   Management systems to sustain progress.

Visual control: You need to see problems and abnormalities as close to real time as possible so they may be resolved in a timely manner. Visual controls are communication tools designed to create transparency and provide immediate, visual feedback on operational status. These tools include production boards that track output against targets, andon lights that signal problems, kanban cards for inventory management, shadow boards for tool organization, and floor markings to designate work zones. Other common controls include standard work instructions with visual aids, 5S color-coding systems, and visual performance metrics that display real-time key performance indicators (KPIs). The fundamental purpose of these controls is to make abnormalities immediately apparent so issues can be addressed quickly, while also standardizing processes to reduce variation. Effective visual controls require minimal interpretation, allowing anyone—regardless of language barriers or experience level—to understand workplace status at a glance, ultimately supporting continuous improvement efforts by making waste visible.

Sticking a management report or microscopic Excel file on the wall is not visual control. In fact, if no one is paying attention, it may do more harm than good. Visual control charts need to be easily read from a distance. Communicate the goal and show a trend. For example, if a goal is at least 90 percent, I am much more concerned if we're at 90 percent now but had been at 95 percent, than if we're at 90 percent and started at 80 percent.

Leader standard work: Defining the key tasks and activities that leaders at all levels of an organization must perform to support excellence and improvement. If we can have standards for the people who do the work, we must have standards for the leaders.

The journey toward a dynamic, holistic business system requires relentless focus on waste elimination, adherence to fundamental principles, and robust management systems. As demonstrated through diverse examples—from manufacturing breather drains to processing insurance claims—organizations that empower employees to question processes, implement visual controls, and standardize work can achieve remarkable transformations. The power lies not in complex solutions but in simple, practical approaches: replacing unnecessary rust-proofing with a used dishwasher, turning insurance claims into "one and done" experiences, or eliminating wasteful waiting for police reports. Success comes when leadership commits to spending significant time on people development, when visual management makes problems immediately apparent, and when everyone embraces the philosophy that standardization creates the foundation for continuous improvement. By integrating these principles, organizations can dramatically reduce lead times, improve customer satisfaction, and create sustainable competitive advantage in any industry.

Chapter 4

Honor the People Who Do the Work to Improve the Work

Creating value for employees starts with respect, which typically takes many forms. The experiences to follow highlight how a holistic business system includes all these practices:

- Involvement in problem-solving and decision-making
- Clear expectations and responsibilities/standard work

- Training and resources necessary to be successful
- Willingness of management to observe firsthand the struggles
- Listening with intent
- Fair compensation
- Safe and decent work environment

"We kill people with our trucks." Not the answer I expected when the value stream analysis workshop team asked the transportation manager what the biggest problems were. It is an understatement to say that accidentally killing people is not a safe work environment. Fortunately, the team had a countermeasure.

This occurred at a company, located in Asia, which is one of the world's largest producers of pulp and paper. Trees were cut, trucked to the mill, staged, and processed into pulp. The pulp was either shipped to customers who made paper or to their own on-site paper fabrication facility. Pulp and paper had to be trucked approximately 12 miles to be loaded on a ship. Finally, acacia trees were planted to replace what was cut. The road to port was unfinished, hilly, and winding. The result was that villagers were often hit and killed.

The first item on the value stream improvement plan was to build a new road to the port. The company offered to pay for the road and the government agreed (after all, lives were saved). In addition, transportation time was reduced, as was damage to cargo. The improvement plan identified many initiatives such as improving the planting of trees and just-in-time delivery of the trees to the mill. A common theme across all their workshops was respect.

One of the first workshop teams focused on the process of planting small acacia sprouts. They started by documenting current state. This entailed going to the fields and conducting time observations. The process was to dig a hole, put the tiny sapling in the hole, pack the dirt, fertilize, and water. This process was done by two people, and it quickly became obvious that the work was not balanced between the two people. One person was digging, placing, and packing dirt and the other was fertilizing and watering. The person who was fertilizing and watering was always waiting on the person who was digging, placing, and packing.

The problem was obvious to the observer. We asked why they did not divide up the work evenly. They said that was the way they were told to do it. We asked if they would prefer to spread the work evenly between them. They just nodded and smiled.

The workshop team immediately implemented a countermeasure: to rebalance the work by moving the packing of the dirt to the person who was fertilizing and watering. This resulted in an immediate 20 percent productivity improvement. Multiply this by planting 300 million trees a year and the results were staggering.

The momentum from listening to those who did the work was infectious. Respect was demonstrated by involving the planters in problem-solving and decision-making, setting clear responsibilities and work instructions, willingness of management to observe firsthand the struggles of the planters, and listening to a simple improvement that had huge benefits.

Building on this success, another workshop team focused on the massive inventory of cut trees. Outside the mill there were many acres of cut trees waiting to be processed.

Inventory is always waste even if it is in trees. How long a cut tree was in the yard impacted the quality of the pulp produced. There were so many trees they had to sleep for days before they were used.

The root cause (pun intended) was not the number of trees but the schedule for cutting. The workshop team asked questions until they were satisfied that they understood the real problem.

- Why is the pulp poor quality?
  - Trees are aged.
- Why are they aged?
  - Too many trees in yard?
- Why so many trees in yard?
  - Trees are cut as fast as possible.
- Why cut so fast?
  - No link between those who cut the trees and their customer, the mill.

The countermeasure was for the mill to notify the tree cutters how many trees they would be processing per day for the rolling next two weeks. The trees could only be cut to keep up with demand from the mill. No overproduction was allowed.

Again, the results were huge, and management had growing recognition that a little respect goes a long way.

During a later visit to this producer of pulp and paper, I was invited to be a judge for a competition regarding the best kaizen (workshop) of the year. I was apprehensive because all improvements should be recognized and rewarded.

It turned out the competition was for children in middle school. They were doing kaizen!

One of the teams that was recognized had solved a problem regarding congestion in the hallways between class that caused students to get to their next class late and also caused breakage of vases that decorated the halls.

The team documented the current state by doing spaghetti diagrams of several students as they walked from class to class. A spaghetti diagram is a visual representation that tracks the movement of people, materials, or information through a process or physical space. The name comes from the appearance of the finished diagram, which often resembles a plate of tangled spaghetti due to the many crossing lines. It was obvious from the diagrams there was no pattern to walk the corridors.

The students brainstormed defined traffic lanes and simulated the result. Implementation included visually indicating the flow of traffic and training all students. Students may still be occasionally late for class; however, it's not because of congestion.

Their smiles at the award presentation said it all. Although it has been many years, I can still feel the energy in the room. They had been trusted with solving a problem and implementing a solution. They created a standard and provided training for all students to follow. They tracked the results to ensure that their fellow students had it a little easier. They demonstrated that everyone should be empowered to improve their circumstances. My time with this company was a moving experience. A continuous improvement journey can truly create value beyond the income statement.

We made these changes based on a greater belief not just in the lives of the workers, but their inputs into the quality of their work. This shift was enabled by our focus on preserving the safety of the people doing the work, as well as relying on their expertise in implementing positive changes.

This approach starts with a management approach defined as being present, observing the work being done, and listening to the people doing the work. This is the heart of the business system and greatest contributor to value creation. Above all, showing respect promotes a culture where improvement comes from the ground up, which is most impactful.

Management is responsible for accountability. However, management often does not provide the standard work, training, and tools to be successful. Holding someone accountable without these management systems is the ultimate disrespect within the business system. Listening to the people who are doing the work and seeking their input is essential for building effective standard work, training, and tools. Holding individuals accountable for results in a responsible way is a primary form of showing respect, as well as providing management systems enabling them to thrive.

I first learned about an improvement business system at Crouse-Hinds. I had a mentor at Crouse-Hinds, Bill Tuck, who exposed me to several distinct roles in the business. I was a financial controller, a supply chain manager, a sales manager in the Northeast, and a plant manager. It was in my role as a sales manager that I first learned about improvement systems.

Our largest client at the time was Wiremold, which makes protective covers for wiring called electrical raceways. If you want to install a plug and not have to cut into your wall, you could run a raceway along the wall and run the electric through it. The plugs that were used in the raceway were Crouse-Hinds Arrow Hart manufactured. Wiremold was our largest customer.

When I was making a sales call with our salesperson, we would go out on the floor and meet with the people who used the plugs in assembly and ask if they had any issues. This was at Wiremold's request. This was a memorable experience learning the importance of showing up and seeing the work being done and listening to the people who do the work. This would be reinforced throughout my journey, and has become the central theme to my leadership style.

I was on the floor, talking to the people who were using these plugs and receptacles, and there was a lot of commotion going on at the factory. I asked, "What's going on?" And they said, "The damn consultants are here." They said it kind of knowing that these people were really helping them but at the same time they were really challenging them. It was a powerful relationship. That was the first time I met Chihiro Nakao, who was there facilitating a kaizen. I saw what was going on and I met Art Byrne at that time. Art has been a longtime mentor throughout my journey. This was really my first exposure to continuous improvement. Wiremold had good visual management; you could look at the visuals and see significant improvement going on. I came back to Crouse-Hinds with this idea that maybe we should learn about this process and apply it at Crouse-Hinds. Art offered to introduce us to Bill Moffitt.

I invited Bill Moffitt of Moffitt Consultants, a company I would eventually lead, to visit us in Syracuse. Bill Moffitt worked at Danaher and with Sensei Nakao and Art Byrne.

When Bill visited Crouse-Hinds, the very first thing he did was tour with Bill Tuck and me. We had a million square feet, 700 employees, and traditional functional manufacturing areas. All the CNC lathe machines were in one area and the screw machines were in another, and then there was this monument to wash and then this other monument to plate, and then a separate area for assembly.

A monument is something that's centralized that all products must go through. For example, there was only one wash system in the entire company. All this machining is happening, and then all parts get queued up in front of this washer because after you cut chips or do machining, there's oil on the parts and they must be washed. All the parts that need to be washed had to wait their turn in front of this monument, creating a choke point.

The batch process entailing large quantities going through functional areas that are all spread out meant that it took months to create a product. We were manufacturing electrical construction materials, and the actual time making a particular product might have been 30 or 40 minutes spent touching/producing the product, but these 30 or 40 minutes were spread out over months because of the time it took the parts to move in batches through these functional departments and monuments.

A few minutes into the tour, Bill Moffitt stopped to tell Bill Tuck that "Everything is Wrong". That conversation could have gone in two different directions. Bill Tuck could have said, "Well, you don't understand. This is not the automotive industry. This isn't Wiremold. This is not Danaher. We make a different product." He could have gone into excuse mode or into blame mode. But instead of Bill making excuses or assigning blame, he said, "Show us. Let's give it a try."

That's really an attitude within continuous improvement that you must have. You must be willing to learn and to try new things. That was a defining moment because Bill Tuck chose to learn and give it a try. In that moment he was letting go of top-down problem-solving and empowering us to make a difference.

Understanding what motivates individuals is another element of showing respect. It is especially important when facilitating a workshop to understand the motivation of each team member.

I learned this in an uncomfortable way personally. When we created the value stream business units at Crouse-Hinds, we needed to assign a manager to supervise each unit. I promoted our best engineer to serve as the manager of one of these units. After a few months this employee—our most effective engineer—left the company. I couldn't understand why he chose to leave. He had a great team and all the training and resources he needed to be successful. I ran into him a year after he left and asked him why he left. He explained, "I got put into this management position and it was a lot of responsibility, stress, and I couldn't get home to my kids at the end of the day. I just wanted to be an engineer." I assumed that because I wanted to get to the next level in my career that everyone else had similar goals. I learned that people are motivated differently. I had failed to realize that.

Another workshop example from the transformation at Crouse-Hinds took place in the turning machine department. We learned that most people want to do a good job. But lacking the necessary standards, training, and tools to be successful can be demoralizing, disrespectful, and wasteful, and highlights management ineffectiveness.

We started by documenting the current state by performing time observations and completing standard work combination sheets. This is a detailed document that shows the exact sequence of work elements performed by an operator. It combines time elements, work sequence, and movement information into one comprehensive visual tool.

The team discovered that it took a very long time to change the equipment from one type of part to another. As a result, we were running large quantities of parts and storing them. The team concluded that setup reduction would increase capacity and flexibility to produce what the customer needed. This was not a surprise.

What was surprising, however, was learning that the department had far more machinists than needed. When the team took the number of parts the customer required and multiplied that by the time it took to run each part, and considered the time needed for changeovers, we learned that the department only had to produce parts for a small fraction of one shift. The department was running two shifts. The team realized there were 20 more machinists than we needed. This was half the department! The union's response was what took us so long to figure this out. As plant manager, I was embarrassed. Without our management systems (standard work, visual management, leader standard work) I was not doing my job nor being respectful. I also learned that human nature is to look at the work that must be done and the time allocated to do the work and pace accordingly.

Our coach for the workshop recommended we show respect and not lay off anyone in the aftermath of this workshop. We moved the freed-up machinists to our improvement office to work on other improvement opportunities. We also formalized a policy that no one would lose their job because of improvements made. We eventually realized the productivity gains by redeploying the extra machinists to support growth and fill retirements.

Over the course of my career, I have led many staff reductions for economic reasons. I have never been associated with a layoff resulting from improvement activity. Why would anyone be involved with improving a process if it resulted in losing their job or a coworker being laid off? Workers would refuse to participate and the prospects of identifying breakthrough improvements would flame out. The ability of an organization to implement this business system would cease. I have seen it too many times. I've learned that it's far better to show respect by not laying off anyone because of improvement.

Another company that exemplified respect is a national mattress retailer. When they developed their version of this business system they had a few hundred locations. In 2024 they had thousands of locations and value creation of several billion dollars. On their operational excellence journey, they focused improvement activities on every process in their order-to-cash value stream.

They started with a value stream analysis and improvement plan. From a retail standpoint they appeared to be a very simple business. No manufacturing—they just sold mattresses. I have participated in over 50 value stream analysis workshops, and this simple business identified over 190 opportunities for improvement, the most I have ever experienced. Over the next few years, they held workshops in every part of the business.

Their strategy deployment focus was to develop efficient processes that were scalable and repeatable to support their high-growth strategy. This entailed setting clear expectations and responsibilities and standard work everywhere.

One of the first workshops was focused on reducing the financial impact of high fuel surcharges. At the time, gas prices were high and rising. The trucking company that delivered and set up the mattresses was charging a surcharge to offset their rising fuel costs. Management believed there was nothing they could do about it because gas prices were high, but they said, "Let's give this workshop stuff a try." We pulled a team together that combined employees who did the work with some fresh eyes. The first day the team went to the warehouse to see the shipping and delivery process.

The workshop team observed the work being done and listened to the people doing the work. As we watched the mattresses being loaded onto the trucks, we saw that a truck was loaded with a few mattresses and left partially full. Then a few more mattresses were loaded onto another truck, and it left. This was repeated until all the deliveries went out. Someone asked why the trucks were going out half-empty. The material handler said, "I see how many trucks are sent to me and I spread out the work." He wanted all the drivers to get some work.

Now, the third-party trucking firm charged a fixed cost per truck per day. They got paid on a per-delivery basis. With only a few deliveries per truck, the third-party trucking company was barely breaking even. As a result, they were trying to make up for the difference with extra-large fuel surcharges. It took only a few minutes observing and listening to the material handler to determine the root cause and propose a countermeasure. The plan was to reach out to the trucking company each night and request the number of trucks they would need the next day, ensuring that all trucks would be sent out full. Not only did that eliminate the fuel surcharge, but they negotiated a reduction in per-delivery cost, which resulted in a $500,000-plus annualized cost reduction. Both companies benefited, and once again a problem that was perceived to be "unsolvable" was solved.

It's important to point out that no one was blamed for the trucks not going out full. Respect entails focusing on the process and not on the person. Processes go awry for many reasons. Instead of assessing blame, we focused on finding the root cause and developing countermeasures. The material handler was trying to do a good job. Direct observation and listening to the material handler led to a win for the workers, the company, and a key supplier. This is another of the many ways to show respect.

Another area of opportunity (out of the 190-plus) identified in the improvement plan was accounts payable. The business was growing rapidly, which meant the number of payments the A/P department had to process went up substantially. Staffing had not grown accordingly. Defects were up and morale was down.

The workshop team started as usual with understanding the current state by observing the work being done and listening to the people who do the work. It was a traditional triple-matching process of the purchase order, the receiving document, and the invoice.

After matching, the accounts payable staff would get those three documents (PO, receipt, invoice) from all over the country, staple them together, and file them. A third of their time was spent keeping track of all this paperwork, mailing it, stapling it together, and filing it—enormous waste of overprocessing.

Team member:	"Why are you doing this?"
Accounts payable manager:	"We are required."

Team member:	"Who required it?"
Accounts payable manager:	"The controller."
Controller:	"I don't require it. Check with the CFO."
CFO:	"I don't need it. Probably the outside auditor/ accountants for audit purposes."
Auditor:	"Nope, just have access to them if needed."
Accounts payable manager:	"Doesn't the Sarbanes-Oxley Act require it?"
Facilitator:	"Show me where SOA says that?"
Accounts payable manager:	"Nope, it's not SOA."

After seeing the Sarbanes-Oxley excuse challenged several times, I've learned that no one has ever successfully succeeded in identifying language that dictated there was only one way to meet requirements.

Needless to say, the accounts payable department stopped the unnecessary filing, which was a waste of overprocessing. The warehouse kept the receiving documents. Purchasing maintained the purchase orders. Accounting maintained the invoices. If there was a problem, the documents could be easily located for resolution. By now, I'm sure everything is stored electronically to further improve the process. The result was freeing up one-third of each person's time, so no additional employees had to be hired. Morale and productivity soared.

This all resulted from the accounts payable workshop team observing the work being done, listening to those who were frustrated, including them in problem-solving and decision-making, and setting clear expectations with time-based standard work. Yes, even office functions can benefit from standards that are time based.

It always pays to get the real story from the people doing the work. We saw this at another workshop, in partnership with a supplier who makes viscoelastic (i.e. foam) mattresses.

Their technology was transforming the industry and was becoming a major offering of the mattress retailer. During a value stream analysis and planning workshop the sales team shared that they could sell a lot more mattresses if they just had them in stock. The mattress manufacturer said they had no open orders or backlog, and on-time delivery was nearly 100 percent, according to their scorecard. So why didn't the salespeople have the mattresses they needed in stock at their stores?

The workshop team that investigated this question consisted of stakeholders from both the mattress retailer and the manufacturer. As organizations mature with implementing their business system, it is common practice to extend out to suppliers and customers with joint workshops. A workshop at a supplier's facility delivers direct benefits by addressing inefficiencies at the source. This collaborative approach improves quality, reduces lead times, and lowers costs that benefit both organizations. On-site work reveals hidden constraints and opportunities for standardization or logistics improvements that reduce waste throughout the supply chain. When suppliers experience the benefits firsthand, they typically continue implementing improvements independently, creating sustained value for all their customers.

When the joint workshop dug into the details (process mapping), they learned that if a partial order was received at the mattress retailer, instead of creating a backlog status for the past-due product, the procurement person was canceling the backorder portion of the purchase order and creating a new order for the past-due mattresses. This means the mattress manufacturer never had past-due orders. The procurement person just thought it would be easier and cleaner to close orders with a backlog and only have open orders.

The countermeasure was to stop canceling backorders and to make the past-due orders visible to the mattress manufacturer. Everyone was now aware that the needed mattresses were not available for sale. This led to an order fulfillment workshop at the mattress manufacturer and, over time, the improvement in inventory management led to tens of millions of dollars in additional sales. This is another case where the countermeasure was obvious once the current state was really understood. In this workshop, respect was extended to the supplier by involving them in problem-solving and decision-making. Management at both companies was each willing to observe firsthand the struggles of the other.

Other improvements at the mattress retailer included reducing the time it took to open a new store by 20 days and reducing customer returns by 34 percent. Overall, billions in value creation were realized for employees, customers, and owners.

Of course, showing respect entails accountability and the expectation that when provided the opportunity to do their best work, people will step up and do it. At one company I led we had suggestion boards throughout the facility because we wanted to "listen" to the workers. Around Martin Luther King Day, we got a suggestion that in observance of that day, we should take some time off during the workday and watch videos about MLK. Seems like a great idea; however, the unfortunate supervisor who got this suggestion did not have the authority to act, so the worker jumped to the conclusion that management was not listening. What the suggestion system should have asked is whether the workers had any ideas to eliminate waste from their job or make their job easier, more productive, or safer. We did not define the parameters for improvement activities.

Empowerment does not mean trying to figure out your job each day; that's chaos. Empowerment is being able to make changes to the standard of how the work is being done. A worker must follow the standard work every time. They do not get to deviate, because we want consistent quality, productivity, customer experience, and safety. "But wait a minute—I have a better way." Great, let's listen to the person doing the work and change the standard and that will be the way forward. The cumulative business impact of respect is enormous as you realize countless base hits by the people who do the work, which add up to winning the game. Eventually, we did create a separate process to capture ideas beyond eliminating waste, and the MLK videos were very popular.

Throughout this chapter, we've seen how honoring the people who do the work is not merely a philosophical stance but a practical business imperative. The examples from the pulp and paper company in Asia, Crouse-Hinds, and the national mattress retailer demonstrate that respect manifests in multiple dimensions: listening to workers, involving them in problem-solving, providing clear standards, offering necessary training and resources, and creating safe working environments.

When management takes the time to observe work first-hand and genuinely listen to those performing it, remarkable improvements emerge. From rebalancing tree-planting tasks to optimizing truck loading, from eliminating unnecessary paperwork to improving supplier relationships—these "base hits" accumulate into game-changing results. In each case, the solutions weren't complex or expensive; they simply required respecting workers' knowledge and empowering them to improve their processes.

This respect-centered approach creates a virtuous cycle. Workers feel valued and engaged, leading to better problem-solving. Improved processes reduce waste and increase productivity. Customers receive better products and services. The business becomes more profitable and sustainable. Perhaps most importantly, the culture shifts from top-down problem-solving to a more collaborative environment where everyone contributes to continuous improvement.

The lesson is clear: Empowerment is about giving workers the authority to improve standards within defined parameters. When people understand their role in the larger system and feel respected for their contributions, they become active participants in creating value rather than passive executors of tasks.

As we move forward, remember that the most powerful insights often come from those closest to the work. By honoring these individuals—not just with words but through actions that demonstrate genuine respect—organizations can unlock tremendous potential for improvement and value creation that benefits employees, customers, and owners alike.

Chapter 5

Fix the Problem at the Source to Ensure Quality, Delivery, and Service (and Not Just Cost-Cutting)

Why are so many cars parked at the end of the assembly line? That was the question I asked when I visited a well-known manufacturer of automobiles that was a customer of a company I was managing at the time. I was told the autos were staged at the end of the assembly line until highly experienced technicians inspected and fixed all the defects. This manufacturer of automobiles was legendary for the quality of their vehicles. Although they were shipping quality vehicles, it seemed it was at great expense, meant longer delivery times, and was disrespectful of the workers.

Contrast this with a visit to Toyota, which was also a customer. When the automobiles came off the assembly line, they were driven straight out of the building for delivery—and not staged for inspection. We were a supplier to Toyota and a repeated recipient of Supplier of the Year award. They were eager to share how they checked for adherence to standards at every step of the manufacturing process. If necessary, they would stop production to fix the problem and ensure it could not reoccur.

The goal was to prevent defects in the first place. They knew when the car came off the production line it met their quality standards. Not having to park the car for inspection and repair reduced costs, improved delivery, ensured quality, and did not waste workers' time fixing defects. They knew that keeping the work flowing had to be a better way.

A primary goal of a holistic business system is to prevent defects from happening in the first place. Identifying and addressing quality issues at their point of origin makes powerful common sense for several reasons. Workers are empowered to take responsibility for the quality of their work, preventing defects from occurring. Fixing quality issues after the product or service has been produced just adds cost. A reworked product is never as good as a product made right the first time.

Stopping the process at the first sign of any defect helps quickly identify and correct the cause of what has gone wrong. This is true for any process: manual assembly line, automated assembly machines, machining, transportation, order entry, accounts payable, and so on.

This fundamental orientation toward built-in quality also contributes to building a culture of continuous improvement. Fixing defects at final inspection (rather than when they occur) makes it difficult for root cause identification and preventing the defect from ever happening again. Learning to correct matters at the source builds awareness of how things are being made and establishes a baseline for making them better.

Moreover, this counteracts a major source of waste that erodes competitiveness: focusing primarily on cost-cutting instead of quality and delivery, which unfortunately is epidemic. Such an approach leads to a short-term high at the expense of long-term value creation. Don't get me wrong: costs should, over time, decline when things are being made right. But excessive emphasis on cost-cutting above all else can lead to inferior materials, insufficient workforce, and shortcuts. All of these impact our primary value drivers of quality, delivery, and service.

A cost-cutting mentality leads to quick fixes as opposed to business-system-based countermeasures. Focusing on the bottom line distracts workers from the issue at hand and distracts folks from fixing what really matters. Merely seeking better numbers discourages innovation through lack of investment in new technologies and workforce development. It demoralizes employees with the generally associated "work faster" culture. Cost-cutting ultimately rules out any productive reflection on dramatically improving delivery by training one's eyes away from the work at hand.

I have conducted many voice-of-the-customer workshops where we have listened to and collected unfiltered information about a product or service. The hypothesis of management before hearing from the customers is usually "price is most important." But that's never been borne out as one of their top concerns; "price," in fact, was usually prioritized by the customer after quality, delivery, and service.

I experienced the benefits of moving from a cost-cutting focus to applying a holistic business system that prioritized quality and on-time delivery at a manufacturer of industrial HVAC equipment that I was newly leading. After years of aggressive cost-cutting, this company was still losing money and dealing with a demoralized workforce.

The value stream analysis exposed an opportunity to rethink our approach to quality. This producer of HVAC equipment had 11 production lines. A workshop team conducted a current state analysis and saw that at the end of each line, an inspector tested the units and fixed many defects. This seemed like a suboptimal way to build quality into the products. Our coach challenged the team to develop a system to produce equipment so that only good units came off the line. The countermeasure we used to reduce the number of defects that made it to the end of the assembly line was to have everyone on the line responsible for checking something critical related to quality from both the previous operation and from their own work. With quality checks throughout the process, at the source, only units with no defects would come off the line.

To implement this intervention, the team created standard work that was time-based, actionable by the people doing the work, at point-of-use, and most importantly reflected quality and safety. Everyone was trained in the new standard work and given the opportunity to make additional improvements to it. Assemblers were given the authority to send an assembly back if it did not meet the standard. The attitude shifted from "not my problem" to "everyone owns the final product." Over time, the inspector position at the end of the line was eliminated and the inspectors were redeployed to value-add jobs and quality issues were almost eliminated.

Overall results at this HVAC equipment manufacturer—from creating a version of this business system and implementing it—meant a 40 percent increase in on-time delivery and 90 percent decrease in quality issues. This subsequently drove a 15 percent increase in sales and profits.

Instilling a quality-first approach to work naturally results in superior delivery of quality products and services and fosters a culture of ownership and improvement. Committing to getting it right the first time always leads to improved quality and delivery at the end of the line. I initially learned "It's about quality and delivery, stupid," at Crouse-Hinds. Creating a culture around quality, flow, and on-time delivery based on taking the time to fix problems as they showed up were the true drivers of growth and profits.

One of the products Crouse-Hinds produced was electrical fittings. To look at issues of poor quality, delivery, and productivity, we assembled a workshop team to focus on the assembly machine. The machine assembled electrical fittings, used to attach lengths of conduit pipes together. Each fitting consisted of several metal parts and screws. The workshop team determined the current state by sorting through a large bin of fittings attached to the assembly machine. One out of three fittings introduced by the assembly machine had defects.

Our mentor asked the team if they knew where in the machine the problem was occurring. The team had no idea. This reflected a lack of granular knowledge about how the product was being made. Our mentor challenged the team to figure out how to stop the machine when a quality issue developed so the operator could fix the problem and determine how to prevent the problem in the future. The ideal result from this would be that only high-quality parts would go into the bin.

With a bit of creativity, quality checks were added throughout the machine so it would stop if a defect was detected, and the issue was resolved. It took several weeks to get it fine-tuned but in the end we had almost no fittings going into the bin with quality issues. Inventory levels were reduced by 50 percent, defects reduced 15 percent, and customer service set records.

Contrast this with another scene, where there were barrels of broken glass everywhere. Our workshop team was focused on a machine that made lightbulbs. Raw materials went into the front end of several linked automated machines and packaged lightbulbs came out the end. The operators were measured by the speed and amount of time they could run the machine.

Near the end of the machine, the lightbulbs were provided with energy to see if they were working. If they lit up they would move on to packaging. If they did not light, they would fall into a large barrel underneath the machine. Hence there were barrels of broken lightbulbs everywhere. There were so many barrels of broken glass that we ran out of space. In fact, we estimated that 30 percent of the raw materials never made it to a working lightbulb. Enormous waste. Staring at the barrels, we had no idea why the lightbulbs were scrapped.

Again, we tackled the problem at the source. The workshop team decided to stop the defective lightbulbs from falling into barrels so analysis could be done to determine why the bulb did not light. Turned out there was no standard for calibration between or during shifts.

Standard work was created, and everyone was trained. Standard work is not a "cover your butt" quality policy. First, it must be readily available to the people doing the work. When those who worked the machines were asked if they had work instructions, they said yes. When we asked to see them, they said they were not in the area but in the computer. We asked to see them in the computer, which they said was in another department. When we went to the computer in the other department they had forgotten the password. Finally, they said we could get the procedures from the quality manager.

This set off yet another gigantic red flag: If work standards are not readily available, they certainly will not drive consistent behavior. Hence different operators were setting calibration differently.

Standard work should also reflect quality and safety, be time-based, and be actionable by those who do the work. A high-level policy that states in general terms that the operator should make a part that conforms to all specifications is not actionable. It needs to be specific and understandable to drive consistent behavior. Proper calibration standards led to detection of abnormalities and stopped the machine, and the problems resolved.

The previous culture was "got to keep the machine running to optimize cost." Stopping or slowing the machine seemed counterintuitive. Changing the focus to making only good lightbulbs by fixing flaws in the process not only ensured better customer experience, but also significantly reduced scrap, saving an enormous amount of money.

Again, dealing with problems when they occur rather than waiting to deal with them at the end of the line represents a profound change of mindset with rippling effects throughout production. Improving flow, not leaving work sitting around, can have a huge impact on quality and delivery and therefore create value for everyone involved. It reorients folks naturally in a way that dramatically boosts value cumulatively.

From the role of VP operations, I learned about the benefits of organizing around a value stream to best serve the customer. The company had functional departments such as screw machines, lathes, mills, wash, plating, assembly, and warehousing. It also had administrative silos such as engineering, purchasing, accounting, and marketing.

We created eight business units, organized by product. Each business unit included everything needed to get a product to the customer efficiently. We moved several hundred machines over a few years to accomplish this.

For example, we had a business unit that made explosion-resistant industrial lighting. They got all the equipment needed to make the products in one area and all the support functions dedicated to the team. Everyone was focused on the customers' needs for lighting. By focusing on the product flow, we:

- **Reduced defects:** With parts moving through machining and assembly in one-piece-flow, if a quality issue was discovered, the feedback to the previous step was immediate.

- **Reduced waiting:** Parts moved through the process without having to be queued up.
- **Reduced overproduction:** Shorter throughput time allowed us to make only what the customer was ordering and reduced forecasting.
- **Reduced transportation:** Material only had to move a few feet between the equipment, as opposed to miles across a one-million-square-foot factory.
- **Reduced overprocessing:** Almost all the material handling between departments was eliminated.
- **Reduced inventories by 75 percent:** This was accomplished by building what the customer wanted, and there were fewer quality issues sitting in the warehouse.
- **Reduced operator moving:** Machines were as close as possible to reduce walking.

We ended up improving working capital by tens of millions of dollars. Unfortunately, because of traditional standard cost accounting, this had a negative impact on traditional measures of earnings. Our team learned that when you rapidly bring down inventory as you move to "build-to-order" from "built-to-forecast," overhead is not absorbed and negative variances result. Fortunately, looking at the value streams, the business improved cash flow by over $30 million, and improved quality and delivery contributed to substantial topline growth.

I invested in a company that produced machines that made circular knit fabrics. Almost every hockey sock in North America, for example, is made on one type of these machines. Unfortunately for the textile mills that used these machines, the quality of the sock produced was poor and they had little confidence in purchasing more machines.

If the yarn that fed the machine broke, there was no way to stop the machine before the broken yarn caused a hole in the sock. There was no way to error-proof the process or prevent the defects from occurring in the first place.

Ironically, this problem had been resolved over 100 years ago. Sakichi Toyoda developed an automatic error-detection system for looms in 1896. His innovation was the automatic power loom, which would stop automatically when a thread broke or there was a problem.

This invention became known as the "Type-G Toyoda Automatic Loom" and featured what Toyoda called the "auto-stop" device. This mechanism would detect when a thread broke and automatically stop the loom, preventing the production of defective fabric and allowing a single worker to monitor multiple machines. This principle of "jidoka" (automation with a human touch) was one of Toyoda's most significant contributions and became a cornerstone of the Toyota Production System decades later when his son Kiichiro Toyoda founded the Toyota Motor Corporation. The concept that machines should stop when problems occur to prevent defects was an early precursor to what Shigeo Shingo would later develop into the formal poka-yoke system in the 1960s.

Indeed, the book *Poka-Yoke: Improving Product Quality by Preventing Defects* cites eight principles of basic improvement for poka-yoke and zero defects. First, doing so builds quality into processes by making it impossible to turn out defective products even if an error has been committed. Second, this practice assumes that all inadvertent errors and defects can be eliminated—that mistakes are not inevitable. Third, poka-yoke establishes a culture of "Stop doing it wrong and start doing it right—now!" Fourth, operators generally stop thinking about excuses and shift to a mentality of doing it right, every time. Fifth, this also shifts mindsets from aiming for eternal perfection and instead implementing ideas that improve the current situation immediately by analyzing the situation and thinking of a solution. Sixth, mistakes and defects can be reduced to zero when everyone works together to eliminate them—it is important for everyone in the entire company to work together to eliminate mistakes and defects. Seventh, 10 heads are better than 1—teamwork is the key to effective improvement ideas. And eighth, pursuing genuine poka-yoke solutions for zero defects always orients operators to seek out the true root cause of a problem, using the five why process. It requires that workers get to the root of a problem to ensure that the countermeasure applied is a real solution, and not just a bandage. This results from asking, "Why did the defect occur?" until the true root cause is revealed and the crucial factor can be fixed to prevent the problem from ever recurring.

These circular knit textile machines were an old design and had been around for many years. If the yarn broke it would often result in a flaw in the fabric. The mills were looking for other manufacturers to solve their problem. Fortunately, we learned from Mr. Toyoda's discovery how to prevent defects in the first place or make production error-proof. We used a tensioner device for the yarn to pass through. If the yarn broke it would stop the machine so the yarn could be reattached before a defect could occur.

We undertook retrofitting all the machines we had sold and were in operation. This reinvigorated the sales for this specialized machine and the quality of the socks produced. If you wore a hockey sock recently, it was probably the result of this improved process and great quality and value.

Another experience I had the opportunity to facilitate was conducting many workshops for a global manufacturing company that probably has the largest continuous improvement organization in the world. Even with their capabilities, they relied on outside consultants to drive change.

A workshop at a factory that fabricated metal parts had the objectives of reducing lead times for a family of parts from two weeks to one day while eliminating defects. In determining the current state, the team identified various pieces of equipment around the factory that were available to create a manufacturing cell. The team performed time observations on each piece of equipment to determine runtime or cycle times. Ideally, cycle time at each piece of equipment would equal takt time (Figure 5.1). Unfortunately, there was significant variation. This would make one-piece flow and shortening the lead times difficult.

Having the same equipment as the competition does not give a competitive advantage. But having the ability to modify the equipment to meet specific needs can be a breakthrough. In this case, modifying the equipment to get

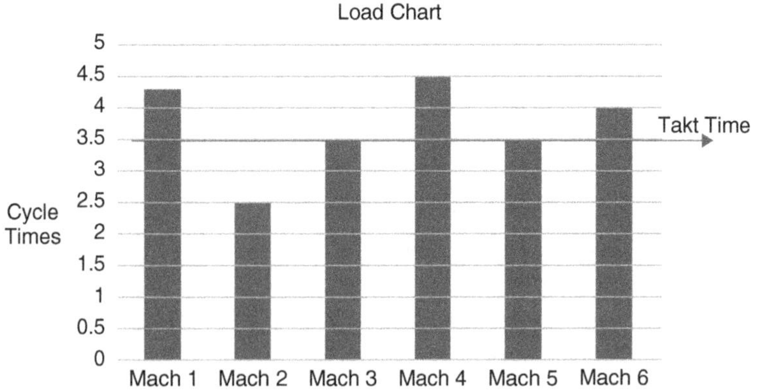

Figure 5.1   Work balance in a flow cell

the cycle time equal to the takt time for all machines became the task. In addition, because the operator moved from machine to machine, modifications were made to have the machine automatically eject the part after it was machined so the operator only had to load parts. A few of the modifications:

- A pneumatic arm was added to a saw to make it semi-automatic, so all the operators had to do was start the cycle and instead of having to manually cut the metal, they were able to start the cutting and move to the next machine.
- Operators built a homemade press that was right-sized to form a very small part.
- Workers ran a track out the side of a CNC machine so a tool could eject the part out of the machine and present it to the operator for loading in the next machine.

The result was producing the product in less than five minutes, down from approximately two weeks, and operating the cell with one operator, down from three. Quality and delivery soared, as did additional business.

Interestingly, in this factory, the union took me aside and showed me on their website that they had their own continuous improvement consultancy. They believed if a company was not successful, they could not negotiate better wages and benefits. They also said that the path to profitability was not cost reduction but being the best at quality and on-time delivery. Wow! If necessary, they would offer their consultancy and help companies improve.

At another company the related focus was on suppliers sharing the same conviction regarding quality at the source. One product, made for the military, was produced on a moving line. The pace of the line is based on takt time. For example, if the customer requires one product a day and there are 20 days of work in one product, then 20 workstations could each have 1 day of work. When the workshop team toured the line, we observed vendor-managed supplies in vending machines. It is not uncommon for consumable supplies to be managed in these vending machines. If an operator needed something, they would get it from the vending machine, and the supplier would be notified of the consumption and would be able to replenish the vending machine, typically on a weekly basis, and invoice the manufacturer monthly.

We observed a drill in the vending machine and asked the operator why they would possibly need a drill when assembling what was probably one of the most demanding and expensive products in existence. The operator said, "Sometimes the parts don't line up and we have to redrill the holes so we can assemble." Unbelievable. This was our country's leading technology and they were forcing parts to fit. The supplier was not holding tolerance on the parts, and they were out of specification.

It became necessary to go back to the supplier and evaluate their quality systems. Guess what? The deficiencies resulted from the supplier's cost-reduction program. Fortunately, they were willing to work together to put in place necessary error-proofing and quality at the source system. Wow, even the most sophisticated manufacturing in existence has numerous opportunities for improvement.

Focusing on fixing problems at their source rather than at the end of the line represents a fundamental shift in thinking about quality, delivery, and service. As we've seen through numerous examples—from Toyota's assembly line to textile machines, from HVAC equipment to lightbulb manufacturing—this approach consistently delivers superior results across industries and applications.

Quality at the source creates multiple benefits. When workers are empowered to identify and address quality issues where they occur, the entire system improves. Defects decrease, delivery times shrink, costs naturally fall, and worker engagement rises. The contrast between the automobile manufacturer staging cars for inspection versus Toyota's flowing production line perfectly illustrates this principle.

Cost-cutting alone is a flawed strategy. Organizations that focus primarily on cost reduction often create more problems than they solve. As we've seen repeatedly in voice-of-customer workshops, customers prioritize quality, on-time delivery, and service above price. When companies orient their systems around these value drivers rather than merely cutting costs, they create sustainable competitive advantages.

Standard work must be practical and accessible. Work standards that aren't readily available at the point of use, that aren't time-based, or that aren't actionable by the people doing the work won't drive consistent behavior. Effective standard work becomes the foundation for quality and the baseline for continuous improvement.

Value stream organization aligns with customer needs. Organizing work around product families rather than functional departments dramatically improves flow, reduces waste, and creates responsive systems that can quickly adapt to customer demands. Though traditional accounting systems may initially struggle to capture these benefits, the improvements in working capital, quality, and delivery ultimately drive substantial growth.

Error-proofing is both mindset and method. From Sakichi Toyoda's automatic loom to modern poka-yoke systems, building quality into processes by making defects impossible represents a powerful paradigm shift. This approach requires everyone in the organization to believe that zero defects are possible and to work collaboratively to achieve them.

The companies that thrive in competitive markets are those that have learned to build quality into their processes, not inspect it in at the end. By focusing on addressing problems at their source, organizations create systems that naturally deliver higher quality, faster delivery times, better service, and, ultimately, stronger financial performance.

The path forward is clear: fix problems where they occur, empower workers to own quality, organize around value streams, and build systems that make it impossible to produce defects. When organizations commit to these principles, they discover that quality and delivery—not cost-cutting—are the true drivers of sustainable success.

Chapter 6

Prioritize Learning as the Fundamental Source of Continuous Improvement

At a company I led, a subcommittee of our board of directors reviews key improvement initiatives. Fortunately, a longtime mentor, Art Byrne, leads this committee. We have a factory in Canada that produces downhole tools for the energy industry. Several years ago, lead times were eight weeks and on-time delivery was poor. Although we had tens of millions in inventory, it was not what the customer was buying. Inventory turns were less than two times. The board visited the facility and helped set the goal to build what the customer wanted, when they wanted it, in less than one week. Satisfy the customer from fast production rather than from finished good inventory.

Most of our workshops involve trying countermeasures and adjusting based on what was learned. During a workshop the team reflects on what worked, what did not work, why it did not work, and what could be done differently next try.

Many workshops were held to improve flow. During each workshop, changes were tried. The teams evaluated what worked and what didn't. Changes were made and we tried again. The board committee held quarterly calls and periodically visited the factory to reflect with the team on lessons learned from the changes.

One workshop focused on a saw that was located at the opposite end of the building from where the steel bar was located and the next operation of drilling. This required the material to travel the length of the facility to be cut, travel to storage, and then travel back the length of the facility to be drilled. The workshop team moved the saw next to the material and the drilling machine, thereby eliminating the need to travel back and forth the length of the facility.

This significantly reduced the travel distance. However, at the 90-day review, there was no reduction in throughput or lead time. Upon reflection, the team discovered that instead of the material moving from the saw to drilling, it was traveling to a storage area to wait a few days for the drilling machine to be available, which did not reduce throughput time. Instead of considering it a failure, the team figured out how to balance the work so the steel bar could flow directly from the saw to the next step of drilling. Three to four days were reduced from the lead time.

Over the years at this manufacturer of drilling tools, the attitude of try, learn, and adjust has reduced the lead time from eight weeks to two weeks. Inventory reduced dramatically. The goal is still one week, and with the board there is continuous reflection on why the work is stopping.

LEARNING BY DOING

The workshop process itself is a learning incubator. It is not uncommon for a workshop team to have different opinions on how to achieve an improvement. Rather than excessive debate, often it is best to give each of the alternatives a try. Learning from the experimentation usually leads to buy-in from the team and quick implementation.

During my consulting years I was facilitating a workshop to create a work area or cell to produce charging stations for one of the first electric vehicles. The charging station had been designed, but it had never been built. The team brainstormed six or seven different ways to set up the cell. Without arguing about whose cell design was best, the team quickly set up the first idea for a cell and gave it a try. Results were tabulated and the team went on to try the other scenarios. Upon reflection of what worked and what didn't, the team finalized a cell design. In one week, we created a very productive cell and had buy-in from a wide range of workers. The workshop process itself contributed to the culture of learn by doing.

Learning is the most fundamental type of continuous improvement. This mindset informs all our methods and practices, which are designed to generate *operational* learning—lessons and improvements derived from disciplined approaches to uncovering and resolving performance gaps. In everything we do, the underlying goal is to try something out, learn from it, incorporate that discovery into our standard work, and then endeavor how to improve the process anew.

I realized early in my career that transformational change starts with developing people and not with simply using "Lean" tools. During my time with Moffitt Consulting, several companies came to us with similar concerns that they thought they were doing Lean or Toyota Production System or Six Sigma, and it didn't work. We discovered a common contributor to failure was over-reliance on common continuous improvement tools, without understanding that a successful business system is built around people and their development.

When I attend a PowerPoint training class, I probably retain about 15 percent of what is taught. Over my career I have created or amassed thousands of pages related to continuous improvement business systems. They are really good sleep aids. Almost everything I've learned has resulted directly from hands-on experiences and the teams I worked with. When I hire a new executive or manager, the first thing they get is a sign (Figure 6.1).

I remember trying to learn about material replenishment. I asked my mentor for this workshop, Bob Pentland, to give the team the "formulas." He said that there are no formulas and we should figure it out on our own. The team struggled. We decided we did know the lead time to get the parts, the daily usage, and how many came on a skid. After

Time Allocation

People Development

Make Improvements

PowerPoint & Everything Else

Figure 6.1   Desk sign given to every new manager.

deliberation it started to make sense how many to order when inventory got down to a certain point. We asked Bob if we were correct. He just shrugged and walked away. Out of frustration we decided to go back the last 90 days and simulate what we had proposed against actual customer orders. Wow, it worked!

We quickly addressed another part. Unfortunately, because of lumpy customer demand, we missed some customer orders when we ran the simulation. We tried increasing the point where we would reorder and discovered that it worked. Wow again! From the struggle we learned and internalized how material replenishment in this situation works.

Bob did not really care about reorder points or quantities. He cared about developing us so we could solve similar problems ourselves. Today we use AI to size material replenishment systems. However, our consultant, MoffittXL, still requires us to figure it out first on paper before we use digital tools. We are required to learn and understand.

I also discovered that learning as a team can be very powerful. I probably would not have figured out much on my own. Workshop teams usually are diverse in terms of roles and responsibilities. This diversity contributes to better ideas and solutions. Most of what I have learned about improvement activities I learned from fellow team members.

I worked with a workshop team at a company that manufactures specialized equipment. When we went to the assembly area to understand the current state, one of the assemblers said, "Stay out of my area. I don't need that Lean kaizen stuff." The team ended up renovating the adjacent assembly bench. Parts were now filled from the back of the bench and were at the assembler's fingertips. The bench had new lighting and a new comfort mat to stand on. Necessary tools that were missing were purchased and hung on a new pegboard, with outlines of the tools to make it easy to keep organized. The assembler who told us to stay away watched this awesome transformation and said, "Hey, I want those things in my area." The team replied, "Sure, how can we make your job better?"

The assembler told us they learned just about everything they needed to know about their business system from seeing their coworkers being listened to, the changes being made, and the results.

Learning by doing can take many forms. A method that works well for a specific task is a three-step process: (1) Show the task. (2) Show the task and explain the key points. (3) Show the task, explain the key points, and give the reason why. This may need to be repeated a few times until the student is comfortable demonstrating that they learned the task and know the key points and why. Often, a new employee is trained by someone who is very good at doing the job. However, this does not mean they know how to train. Creating a script in this format can be very helpful for workers to have on hand if they need to train someone and can ensure a great learning experience.

Here is an example script for grinding:

Task: Grind—Body

   Key point: Do not press down.

   Reason: Could cause injury from kickback and damage to pad or grinder.

   Key point: Always keep two hands on the grinder: one on handle and the other on trigger.

   Reason: Could cause injury from kickback.

   Key point: Start on one side of rack and work way around the rack.

   Reason: Avoid missing a section of the rack.

   Key point: Keep guard between operator and wheel.

   Reason: To protect operator.

   Key point: Debris trail should not be in the direction of self or anyone else.

   Reason: Safety.

   Key point: Do not reach outside of strike zone.

   Reason: Avoid ergonomic and kickback injury.

Task: Grind—Sharp Edges

   Key points: Remove anything that could cause a cut for an operator.

   Reason: Employee safety.

   Key point: Round all corners.

   Reason: Customer requirement.

Task: Grind—Spatter

   Key Point: Remove in areas of contact by dunnage or customer.

   Reason: Could cause part to not function properly or injury.

Key Point: Try to remove by scraping before grinding.

Reason: Safer to scrape spatter away from Grinder. No risk of swirl marks.

THE BENEFITS OF FLOW

One of the hardest concepts to learn is to make one at a time versus making a bunch (one-piece flow versus batch). I have won many bets over the years that single-piece flow is the least wasteful way to produce. For many workers it feels faster and more efficient to complete similar tasks repeatedly.

In a workshop, I supported an assembler who was taking 25 bases out of a bin and laying them out on the bench. They picked 25 gaskets and placed them on each base. Then they picked 25 covers out of a bin and screwed them to the base. Finally, they placed all 25 bases on a skid to be transported a few feet to the next workstation. The workshop team asked the assembler to try one at a time. Parts were organized so all the assemblers had to do was pick up a base, install the gasket and cover, and hand it to the next operation. The operator learned that one at a time was faster and easier. They also had less risk of missing a step. They were sure the batch way was better until they tried and proved to themselves that flow was the way to go.

One-piece flow outperforms batch processing by reducing inventory, catching defects immediately, and dramatically shortening lead times. This approach reveals inefficiencies more clearly because problems can't hide within batches, making improvement activities easier. Though requiring more frequent changeovers, one-piece flow's benefits of reduced waste, faster throughput, and improved quality typically outweigh these challenges in most production environments. Relentless setup reduction maximizes the benefits.

At a manufacturer of electrical construction materials, learning to trust one-piece flow was an enormous challenge. Their batch process had large quantities going through functional areas that were all spread out, which meant it took months to create a product. The actual time making a particular product might have involved 30 or 40 minutes spent touching/producing the product, but those 30 or 40 minutes were spread out over months because of the time it took the parts to move in batches through these functional departments.

Our teacher, Bill Moffitt, told management they could not fix it themselves. If they did, it would not be accepted by the people who do the work. However, they could teach the people how to do it, and they would learn best by doing. Over three years I probably participated in 30 workshops at this company, and I learned something every time about the process of improvement and, through trial and error, the task itself. Slowly we started to understand the benefit of flow. In fact, 30 years later, I am in workshops just about every week and am still learning about the process of making improvements.

IT'S NOT ABOUT YOUR EGO

The first kaizen (workshop) I participated in at Wiremold was focused on the rolling mill, which is used to form sheet metal into a wall-mounted raceway that provides protection for electrical wiring. When we began the workshop, we learned that initially it took the rolling mill more than an entire shift to transition from one product to another. This long transition time generates significant inventory because you're not going to do a lot of long changeovers. During previous workshops the team had gotten the setup time down to about 15 minutes. Our goal was to get it under 10 minutes. SMED (single-minute exchange of die) is one of the concepts emphasized by Shigeo Shingo, a contributor to the Toyota Production System.

Our team accomplished three things: We eliminated waste, we made the job easier for the operator, and we made the process more flexible to better serve the customer. We were able to reduce the changeover time to seven minutes. Surely, we thought, we were now the best in the world at changing over this type of equipment and ready to show off. The sensei/facilitator for the kaizen, Chihiro Nakao, came out to review our progress. We proudly demonstrated the changeover in seven minutes. He looked at us, said, "Not good enough—five minutes," and walked away.

We realized that this is not about our ego and what a great job we did in achieving our initial results. He wanted us to reflect on the changes and try again. It's about continuing to learn. It's not okay to relax and let up after achieving a good result. Everyone needs to understand what went right, what went wrong, and how to humbly build on this progress by continuing to better understand present state, and to hold that up to ideal state.

We focused on gap analysis to measure the gap between what we were currently doing and what was ultimately possible. The focus is not on how an organization compares to similar organizations. We may be better than the competition and become complacent. They could find a way to leapfrog us in terms of quality, delivery, service, or cost, and suddenly we are losing market share. Organizations need to continually reflect on what is ultimately possible, set break-through objectives, and continuously strive to learn and improve. Chihiro Nakao and Art Byrne taught us to continue to learn about the process, strive for what is ultimately possible, and not be satisfied by being a little better than the competition.

These were also lessons in humility. I had much to learn back then, and I still have much to learn now. In fact, the business system in this book, which is simply a summary of what I have learned, is evolving every day and being customized to meet current needs.

I returned to Wiremold for another president's kaizen and another *lesson in humility*. Our key challenge was to integrate machining, which took place in one area, with assembly, which took place in a separate part of the factory floor. We had to figure out how much we needed to produce on the machining side to support assembly, and how to manage the material replenishment.

How were we going to do that? I had learned about this concept called *kanban* (literally, "sign board"), reportedly developed by Taiichi Ohno at Toyota. In manufacturing, kanban is a method for signaling the need for material replenishment. For example, if an operator needs a part or material, they will take the corresponding card and send it to the machining area. The machining area would then produce it and send it to assembly.

I had learned all about how to calculate the replenishment quantity. You need to know the usage, lead times, and container quantities, and to adjust for variation. Here's a simple example: If it takes five days to produce a part and you need one part a day, you need to place an order when down to five parts or you will run out. I learned all about this material replenishment process (kanban) and did all the appropriate calculations. Now I was going to impress Chihiro Nakao. He came out and we walked to the machining area and then we walked to the assembly area. We then walked back to the machining area and again to the assembly area. Then, without saying anything, he walked away.

I realized then that kanban was not the solution. Kanban is a countermeasure that is needed when poor flow leads to complex inventory management needs. Implementing a complicated kanban system wasn't the process improvement we needed. What we needed to do was improve the flow of the parts through the factory floor. It was really all about learning the importance of flow. We moved the part machining area to the assembly area and produced the part as needed. In addition to realizing that Kanban alone is not a goal, I also learned not to try to impress your sensei with how much you know, because you're always learning. I've been on this journey for over 30 years, and again I learn something from every workshop.

WITHOUT HUMILITY, IT'S DIFFICULT TO LEARN

Without humility it is difficult to learn. I was participating in an off-site management retreat with Art Bryne. On our day off we went skiing. I remember telling Art proudly that I reduced our inventory at Crouse-Hinds using "vendor-managed inventory," a process where we let our suppliers hold the inventory. I think I got close to getting thrown off the chairlift because Art became visibly upset. Art (not so patiently) explained that inventory is always waste. If you're piling up inventory at a supplier, it doesn't matter where that inventory is being stored because you're still paying for it.

Shifting inventory to the supplier was not the solution. The solution was to fix the process so the manufacturer can produce parts just in time when they are needed. That makes sense. When you move your junk from your house to your neighbor's house, it's still junk. Creating an environment where people feel safe to ask questions and challenge the status quo is paramount. It starts with leadership. Although Art was very passionate about my question, I knew his goal for inviting me to the off-site was to learn about continuous improvement. Learn from mentorship.

Once you begin to observe things through a continuous improvement lens, you see potential lessons everywhere. For example, another "lesson learned" happened at a sushi restaurant we visited with Art Byrne and Chihiro Nakao. While sitting at the counter, Art and Chihiro asked me, as an exercise, to explain how sushi orders work. Well, I could see the customers telling the chef what they wanted. The chef—who was always facing me and did not leave the counter—picked up the fish, prepared it, and placed it in front of me. While I was eating, the chef was preparing my next piece. By the time I was done with the first piece, he had put the next in front of me. Meanwhile, his line server would look at what fish has been taken from the tray and quickly replenish it. They said I just learned what I need to know about takt time, one-piece flow, pull system, and material replenishment systems. Learn from observation.

I learned about takt time at a bar. Our teacher for that week's workshop ordered two beers. Having learned about the benefits of one-piece flow, I jokingly "accused" him of batching. His response was to point out that the cycle time (how long it takes the server to get him a beer) could not keep up with what he wanted (takt time). This was a simple example of matching process to customer requirements. Learn from experience.

My best experience with building a business system on the philosophy of developing people was at a family-owned company that makes access products such as basement doors and roof hatches. This company created tremendous value along their improvement journey for employees, customers, and the owners, and is now part of a publicly traded company.

I learned the significance of leadership in developing an organization. The board of directors included former Danaher and Wiremold executives. For most workshops, the CEO attended the kickoff meeting, daily leaders update, and final report-out. He was regularly present in the workplace, observing the work, listening to the people doing the work, sharing their struggles, and coaching how their business system could be used to make improvements. I never saw or heard him telling an employee how to fix a problem. His focus was developing people, building a problem-solving organization, and pointing out waste so others could eliminate. His impact was inspirational and motivating.

Although each factory had fewer than 50 employees, they typically would have over 30 workshops a year at each factory. When they started, they thought every workshop had to be a grand slam. They learned and demonstrated that many small learnings or base hits add up to breakthrough transformation.

The steps in their manufacturing were cut steel, bend steel, weld, paint, and assembly. Before their improvement journey, large numbers of each part (batches) were produced. The opportunity was identified from value stream analysis and improvement plan to produce only the parts needed for one finished product. This would drastically reduce the lead time to produce the product, reduce handling and storage, and identify and resolve quality issues early in the process. To accomplish this, they drastically reduced setups. It was truly world class to be able to cut and bend up to a dozen different parts as needed to support the production of a single finished good. Eventually, this company was acquired by a larger company. Benefits from their improvement journey are confidential; however, they are extraordinary.

Continuous learning is the cornerstone of sustainable improvement. Workshops may be used to drive operational excellence and foster a culture of experimentation, trying countermeasures, reflecting on results, and adjusting processes accordingly. People development is crucial to transformational change. Many companies fail at initiatives because they focus on tools rather than fostering a learning and problem-solving mindset. Practical learning, rather than theoretical training, is most effective, whether through structured workshops, mentorship, or direct hands-on experience.

Learning through trial and error, overcoming resistance to change by demonstrating improvements, and understanding that achieving one improvement should only spark the next challenge. Ultimately, humility and hands-on learning are the most powerful drivers of improvement. It's not about implementing tools for their own sake but about fostering a mindset that continually seeks better ways to work.

Chapter 7

Leverage the Compounding Power of Improvement

Benefits compound—one by one, many by many, inexorably. I discovered this basic truth about the compounding power of improvement when implementing a holistic business system at a company that made parts for the energy industry.

Over a five-year period, the company went from losing money to a net profit margin of 14 percent. (The industry average was approximately 5 percent.) How was this achieved?

It all started with value stream analysis and recognition of their deficiencies. Setting up machines for distinct parts was averaging over 75 minutes per changeover. On their own, each of the changes made to bring about these improvements, and the improvements themselves, seemed insignificant:

- Workshop teams reduced this to under 15 minutes. "So what!"
- Quality at the source was initiated. "Big deal!"
- Standard work and visual management were put in place everywhere. "That's pretty!"

These changes, however, compounded to transform from "build to stock" to "build to order." ("Okay that sounds like a good thing—is it?") Changing to build to order freed up more than $15,000,000 in cash used to fund growth. ("That's good!") This led in turn to first-pass quality yield of 98.5 percent and on-time order fulfillment of 99 percent. This contributed to annual revenue growth of over 12 percent. ("Impressive!") It led to productivity improvements of 4–9 percent per year, which lowered costs, improved profitability, and increased employee profit sharing and satisfaction. ("Now you're talking!")

All the small changes to reduce changeovers, optimize standard work, produce quality at the source, and create visual management set off a chain reaction that contributed to increased sales and profits, creating value, or what's important for employees, customers, and owners. Everyone wins.

Improvement builds on improvement. Knowledge builds on knowledge. Small changes multiply. In football, every play a team makes involves hundreds of micro decisions that contribute to the play. The result of the play is analyzed, and adjustments are made for the next. Each play contributes to the outcome of the game. In baseball, base hits are the main contributor to winning the game. In a holistic business system, many small changes compound to create value for employees, customers, and owners.

If a company has industry-leading quality, delivery, service, and cost structure, they should increase market share and revenue, and do it more efficiently. Applying all the basic principles are the base hits that compound to best quality, delivery, and cost structure, which all add up to breakthrough transformation.

In other words, all the various elements of this system work in concert—in total, cumulatively, and not just reinforcing each other in real time but *over* time as well. Just as money compounds over time, so does the power of workshops generate increasing positive returns to business performance, both quantitively and qualitatively. Establishing a culture where excellence is expected and enabled ensures steadily growing positive results.

Simply cherry-picking and adopting one principle is insufficient for success that grows and builds. Enduring success results from paying attention to and following *all* of the basic principles. Doing so creates a mutually reinforcing culture of success where the pieces eventually pull together and lead to huge and unexpected jumps in performance—which establish a new baseline of success, a set of standards that are nothing more than new milestones on the journey to improved excellence.

This dynamic emerges in both tangible and intangible ways. Tangible results create the conditions for better results—just as weak conditions invariably lead to weak results. Poor quality, say, not only jeopardizes customer loyalty and future sales, but it also directly impacts the bottom line.

As an investor in a manufacturer of parts for the motorcycle industry, we measured parts that must be scrapped on a daily basis. This was very costly for the business. Implementation of their business system resulted in reduced scrape and margin improvement of 3 percent. This released capital that was now available for purchase of new equipment to support sales.

Creating a culture that prioritizes learning produces a shared commitment to *more* learning. As workers make improvements to their jobs and see their ideas implemented, this encourages making more changes and suggestions for improvement. Like a snowball rolling down a hill, change increases and accelerates. When you learn something new, it often helps you understand other related concepts more quickly. Skills enhance other skills. As you improve in one area, it often positively impacts related areas. Habits stack and reinforce.

Good habits tend to support the development of other good habits. An associate at a company I am currently leading texts me a couple of times a month with something she learned or an improvement she made. She is continuously looking for opportunities to learn, eliminate waste, and improve safety. It has become part of her job. Her pride is infectious and indicates how the business system has shaped the culture.

Operationally, making tangible improvements reveals greater opportunities for positive change. A common example of compounding is the impact of reduced changeover times. Shorter changeover times leads to smaller batches. This leads to shorter total time to produce, which leads to a smaller finished goods inventory being needed to meet customer requirements and increased order fulfillment. Less inventory and fewer quality issues frees up cash for operations and investment. I worked with one company that traced almost all of their improvement in key performance indicators back to improving changeover.

Compounding can also work in the wrong direction. Defects can compound into a crisis. I once built a large shed. The foundation was wood 2 × 6's and I was a little sloppy with alignment and the corners. When I tried to frame the ceiling, those small problems in the foundation now manifested as visible gaps. When I tried to build the rafters and ridge beam, I had a disaster on my hands. Those small errors in the foundation turned into a major problem with finishing the shed. So it is with suppliers. If purchased parts or material are not to specification, the deficiency can multiply and carry through to the customer. This requires a company's business system to extend all the way back to suppliers. Workshops at the suppliers may improve quality, delivery, service, and cost structure at both businesses. This promotes partnership, as opposed to an us-versus-them relationship.

For many years I collaborated with a company that achieved double-digit productivity every year. Ask top management how they did it and you will get a vague answer about their great business system. Ask an employee and they will tell you specifically the last changes they made to eliminate waste. Numerous small changes to eliminate waste added up inexorably to double-digit productivity improvement.

Every employee was challenged to make a change for the better every week. Every morning in a huddle or start of the day's meeting, the supervisor would ask if anyone had any ideas to eliminate waste. Ideas were acted upon, standard work was updated, and the number of improvements made were tracked on a whiteboard. Think of 52 improvements a year per employee, multiplied by over 1,000 employees, and it adds up.

Frequent improvements were related to sequence of operations and workplace organization. Standard work identifies tasks to be performed, sequence, and time to complete. In an area with multiple machines or assembly, the balance of work may cause bottlenecks. The workers were encouraged to manage the workload across the team to reduce waiting between tasks. Regarding workplace organization, they were continuously relocating and organizing tools to reduce walking and searching, and to make their jobs more productive. Changes were made on top of changes, over and over again, and documented in standard work.

Everyone knew and expected that at every morning meeting they were going to be asked if they had any ideas to eliminate waste (which includes safety). It was a way of life, and, for some, everything they did during the day was filtered through the lens of seeing waste. Although the workers may have had difficulty seeing how these changes added up to company objectives, they could see immediately how their jobs were getting safer and easier and the quality of the product better. Pride in these improvements certainly leads to continuing to make more improvements.

I worked with an organization that had only 55 employees and they held over 25 workshops a year. This company produces a specific type of air conditioner equipment. Metal is bent, drilled, and painted. Pipe is brazed or joined together.

Units are assembled and packaged. Most workshops were base hits. They were not focused on only big workshops with huge returns on investment. They relentlessly utilized principles in their business system to make small changes.

This company held workshops implementing these changes repeatedly. On their own, each workshop progress was good and tallied some benefit, despite some of the gains seeming to be marginal in nature. However, they added up to breakthrough improvements in quality, delivery, service, and cost structure, which contributed to record revenue growth and profitability.

Many companies think they do not have time for workshops or must wait for a big project like a new enterprise computer system before they start. But at this company, when asked how such a small company could find the time, employees responded, "How could they not?" Their jobs were improving and they continually freed up time to work on more improvements. They could see the impact that applying the principles had not only on their jobs but also on the customers' experience.

An example at this company linking this together started with targets to improve from their strategy deployment to increase working capital by several million dollars. This was to fund acquisition activity. Another target was to improve on-time delivery by several basis points. Their value stream analysis and improvement plan identified many areas for improvement that would impact these objectives for working capital and on-time delivery.

A four-day workshop was held to design the future state layout of the factory. Two machinists, two assemblers, a supervisor, a plant manager, an HR associate, and the CFO took part. Equipment was moved together to keep the work flowing and a moving line was designed for assembly. No improvement happened yet to working capital but they knew where they were going and how they were going to get there.

After the equipment was moved, a roadblock was revealed about how long it took to change a piece of equipment over to another operation. This contributed to large batches and work in process between the machines. Several workshops were held to reduce setup times. With each workshop, a little less work in process was needed and small improvements in working capital and lead time started to manifest.

Many workshops were held to eliminate waste in the value stream, improve workplace organization, document (standard work), and create visual management. Every improvement built on previous improvements and made small contributions to working capital and on-time delivery.

We went on to hold workshops to improve the reliability of the equipment (total productive maintenance) and clarify the workers' role and responsibilities in making sure the equipment was always available to run if needed. Again, many small improvements were built on previous improvements and contributed to increased working capital and on-time delivery.

Add it all up and this company generated enough capital to fund a small acquisition. The company they purchased was a startup from a former employee. This worker had an idea to develop new technology to reduce the sound level when the product was running. This was urgently needed because the noise was so high that the product was just about to be discontinued. Unfortunately, at the time, the company had no way to listen and vet new ideas, so this employee left and did it on their own.

Fortunately, management had changed, and no one cared about the failure to develop this internally. The company with sound reduction technology was acquired and the improved technology quickly incorporated into the product. Sales gradually improved. Eventually, with a few other improvements, this product became a market leader. Another benefit was the improved layout and smaller amount of inventory taking up space, which freed up space to move the new business into the existing facility. The acquired business was located in the area where warehouse racks used to be located.

Next was revisiting strategy deployment and value stream analysis to focus on where to apply the principles and achieve even more value creation for employees, customers, and owners. No end to repeating this cycle.

Compounding can have a particularly large impact (good or bad) on inventory. Reduction in inventory is not the primary goal of this business system, because surplus inventory in the system (and there's always surplus inventory to be found) is simply an indicator of waste in the value stream. Many "experts" in the continuous improvement community preach the importance of reducing inventory, but the true purpose for this goal must be made clear. Companies otherwise misinterpret this goal and make poor decisions just to make cuts, which can lead to irresponsible actions such as adjusting computer programs to not purchase raw material.

What's important to note is that excessive inventory and poor inventory turns are above all indicators of how much waste there is in the value stream. A company with excellent flow, whose production is tied to customer demand, rarely needs a fraction of the inventory cluttering production. The appropriate goal is exceptional customer service. Where flow is poor, the question is how much inventory is necessary to support the customer and how to improve the process so excessive inventory is not needed. The primary focus always needs to be improving order fulfillment by removing waste and not just cutting inventory. With fewer finished goods in inventory, the risk of quality issues sitting in the warehouse is reduced. Their risk of obsolescence is reduced, and handling is less. Capital invested in inventory could have been used for other productive purposes that generate returns such as new equipment to increase production, expanding to new markets, and marketing to improve sales. Inventory also has carrying costs that reduce returns, such as warehouse costs, insurance, transportation, and spoilage.

It can be hard to see how a small change eliminating waste is going to make a difference. In turnaround after turnaround, I have witnessed organizations that are surprised—even gobsmacked—regarding the impact of removing waste, savings that have led to hundreds of millions of dollars in value creation.

A private equity leader I worked with learned the compounding impact of frequent workshops. She did not care what we worked on, just that we were making changes. She knew from experience that, "like going to the gym, your body continues to build on previous workouts and get stronger," so would the portfolio companies thrive. Workshops were required at a regular cadence across the portfolio. Every company had to hire someone with continuous improvement experience to build a similar business system. Consultants were utilized to support internal resources. Together we learned common themes across the portfolio.

Improving one part of a process often automatically improves connected processes:

- Reducing errors in data entry means fewer corrections are needed later.
- Better organization of materials reduces searching.
- Standard work improves both training and execution.

As multiple processes improve, they create multiplicative effects:

- Better quality reduces rework across all stages.
- Improved communication accelerates all collaborative work.
- Documentation of solutions creates reusable templates.

Culture builds momentum:

- Teams become more confident in suggesting changes.
- Resistance to change decreases.
- Problem-solving becomes more proactive.

Freed-up resources can be reinvested:

- Time saved can be used for more improvements.
- Money saved can fund better tools or training.
- Mental bandwidth can focus on higher value activities.

The cumulative impact cannot be understated.

A workshop at a portfolio factory also focused on reducing lead time. They produced semi-custom portable stand-up workstations for hospitals. At the time, because of cost pressures, the workstations were produced overseas. Unfortunately, if an order required customization, the lead time was 12 weeks. The challenge was how to make quickly (one-piece flow) what the customer needed (pull system). Their solution was to stop stocking finished workstations and only stock components. Assembly was moved from overseas to the warehouse in the United States. Workstations were now built to what the customer ordered and delivered in a few days. As a result, lead times were reduced to from 12 weeks to 5 days. There was also a significant reduction in finished goods inventory. This was just another example of how, by reducing lead times, it's possible to provide better customer service with less inventory.

The power of compounding improvements lies not in dramatic, singular changes but in the steady accumulation of countless small enhancements. Like compound interest in finance, the returns from consistent, methodical improvements multiply over time, creating value that exceeds the sum of individual changes. Each workshop, each process refinement, and each employee suggestion builds upon previous improvements, forming a foundation for future growth.

The journey of continuous improvement has no endpoint—it's a perpetual cycle of setting new standards, achieving them, and then raising the bar again. As Peter Senge writes in *The Fifth Discipline*, "In building learning organizations there is no ultimate destination or end state, only a lifelong journey." He describes this dynamic as a "reinforcing feedback system," where small actions can grow into large consequences—where small change builds on itself, and where "whatever movement occurs is amplified, producing more movement in the same direction."

The most successful organizations understand that break-through transformations rarely come from a single revolutionary change. Instead, they emerge from a culture that embraces continuous improvement at all levels. When every employee is empowered to identify and eliminate waste, when teams regularly conduct workshops to refine processes, and when leadership commits to supporting these ongoing efforts, the compound effect becomes unstoppable.

Here are some keys to maximizing process improvement compounding:

- Document improvements rigorously.
- Share learnings across teams.
- Build on successful changes quickly.
- Measure results systematically.
- Maintain improvements to prevent regression.

Companies that embrace this philosophy find that their small, consistent steps toward excellence eventually lead to remarkable leaps in performance, customer satisfaction, and financial results. The key is to start making these improvements today, knowing that each small change contributes to a larger transformation that will compound over time.

Chapter 8

Perfect Your Processes Continuously

Standard work is not created in a vacuum and dictated from on high. It is created by the people who do the work. It starts with observing a process, any process: assembly, machine setup, maintenance, data entry, documentation, administrative, and so forth. Improvements are identified and included in the creation of a detailed standard work document. It is necessary everywhere. I have seen entire businesses managed by relying primarily on two documents: strategy deployment and standard work.

Standard work must be understood as the basis for improvement—and not the strict controls of management over how production must happen. It represents a dynamic, ever-changing understanding of the best-known way to deliver value at the time. When used properly, it represents the most powerful way to ensure continuous improvement.

I supported the creation of many examples of standard work at a company that produced commercial locks. Locks for an office building are surprisingly complicated. Each lock must be opened with a unique key and a master. Each office would have its own key, and maintenance would have a key to open multiple offices.

A workshop team was tasked with optimizing and creating standard work for a lock assembly line. Two observers were assigned to observe and time each assembler. Before observation, the observers spoke with the assembler to let them know the purpose of observation was not to judge performance. The focus was on the process, not the person, and to identify ways to make the process easier and more consistent. Several cycles were observed to identify the tasks performed. Several more cycles were timed, identifying times for each task.

The lowest repeatable times for each task were summarized to create current state standard work. Averages are not used because they would bake in problems. The focus was on the assemblers whose cycle time exceeded the time needed to meet customer requirements or takt time. The team then identified opportunities for improvement and incorporated them into new standard work. The assemblers were asked to try the new standard work and the process of creating standard work repeated. The outcome was that the assembly cell was able to produce at the rate needed to satisfy the customer.

Standard work may be created by a workshop team that is representative of others who do the job. When those who are not included in the creation are presented with new standard work, it is not uncommon for the worker to want to change it before they even give it a try. Typically, the changes they want to make are back to the way they are used to performing the work: their way. It is important to ask them to give it a try before making changes. After they try it, ideas for improvement are welcome. They will have an opportunity to make it even better.

One of my favorite sayings is "The journey is the destination." In sports psychology the trend is not to focus on the end result of winning or standing on the podium, but to focus on the next free throw or making some good turns. This applies to developing a continuous improvement mindset. This frame of mind develops through consistent practice of small, incremental improvements. It arises when you shift from seeing improvement as the final solution to viewing it as the next small step.

The key to sustainable improvement lies not in random initiatives but in establishing standards as a foundation and systematically building upon them. A workshop team targeted better adherence to regulations and productivity for highly specialized insurance claims. For pre-work, they used software to record keystrokes or tasks for several hundred claims. The team reviewed this data and audited a selection of claims. The team also observed four agents processing claims.

It quickly became apparent that agents were processing claims "their own way." Procedures were so high level they were not followed. Many agents had their own "cheat sheets" they were using as work instructions. As a result, adherence and time to process a claim varied widely.

How was the team expected to identify waste and make improvements when everyone was doing it differently? The team decided to use a top performer's cheat sheet as the baseline. They closely observed the way that their top performers went about the work and created and shared detailed work instructions based on these leading practices.

The team then asked the four agents to process claims according to the newly established standard. With every round of processing claims, the team and agents identified problems with the standard and shared ideas for improvement. Revisions were made and another round of claims were processed. This was repeated for several cycles.

After the workshop, the new standard work was distributed to a region to pilot. Agents were trained. Everyone was asked to give the new standard a try and not to deviate. Any ideas that anyone had for improvement were sent to the continuous improvement office. Every month a revised work instruction, with changes noted, was sent out to the pilot team. A selection of claims was audited every week. Adherence and productivity were measured and reported. The suggestions were also tracked.

In very little time, adherence to regulation soared. Average time to process a claim became consistent across all agents and the overall average improved. The perception before the first workshop was that those who were fastest were the best performers, and that the slowest were poor performers. What we discovered was that the perceived fast performers were in many cases skipping steps and the poor performers were doing work that was not necessary. With everyone following the standard, doing the same work the same way, variation in individual average time was reduced. Over time, with hundreds of tweaks to the standard, adherence to regulation was assured and productivity continuously improving. They had developed a problem-solving organization—built off a base, and kept improving.

It is difficult to make an improvement if there is not a standard or baseline to improve on. Standard work represents the current best-known or least wasteful way for performing a process or task. Its use is relevant to any place where work is done, including office functions. It is actionable, time-based, readily available, and reflects quality and safety. Standard work ensures consistent quality, productivity, and safety. The least wasteful way doesn't mean "perfect" but is the most effective method currently identified, serving as a baseline for future improvements. You will find the establishment, sharing, and improving standard work as a crucial factor in all of our sustained improvement efforts.

It's vital that those who do the work participate in creating standard work and ongoing revisions. Everyone must come to follow the standard every time. If they cry out, "But wait a minute, I have a better way!" we respond by saying, "Great, let's try it and if it's an improvement, incorporate it into a revision." This basic idea is so important that when I visit the workplace and see standard work that has not been revised recently, I question if improvements are being made.

A workshop typically starts by observing and documenting the current way work is performed. If multiple people have the same job, it is not unusual for workers to each have their own way to do it, resulting in inconsistent quality, productivity, and customer experience. It may be necessary for the team to pick one way as a base to improve on. The team can select best practices and ideas to eliminate waste from the different workers, apply them to the base, and revise standard work.

Whether someone is working with a team or on their own, there is a path to perfect your processes continuously:

- Observe.
- Listen.
- Identify waste.
- Brainstorm countermeasures.
- Try.
- Reflect/Learn. (This involves assessing improvements made and what could have been done better. Not all change turns out the way we want. In some cases, change can make things worse. We need to acknowledge mistakes and learn from them, and accept responsibility.)
- Revise standard work.
- Repeat, Repeat, Repeat.

I have followed this system in workshops, three weeks a month, for over 30 years and I have never experienced a workshop that did not make at least some improvement to a process—even to processes that had countless improvements already made or seemed impossible to improve.

There is always room for improvement. I often encounter resistance from individuals who claim, "We fixed that process already." But upon closer inspection, it invariably turns out that further improvements are indeed possible—even when things appear to be just fine. Although perfection is ambiguous, it is a destination to strive for. We will never get there, but just maybe we will come close.

Improvements do not always lead to other improvements. They may create a false sense of security, comfort, and superiority. Most breakthrough transformations I have been involved with started with establishing a sense of urgency—a burning bridge. For most people, change is uncomfortable. Yet it is in this state of uncomfortableness that improvements are most transformative and a holistic business system most successful.

A burning bridge can bring a team together to set stretch goals, conduct frequent workshops, and reward trying new ways of doing things. Focus is on the process, not the person, and on improvements, not blame.

And then there's daily improvement where a culture of continuous improvement leads people to look at the work and continuously make improvements.

Empowerment is the process through which workers gain greater control of their job. And what better way for individuals to gain more control of their job than to ruthlessly examine how they are going about doing it, casting a critical eye on every aspect—seeking the most tangible ways of doing it better?

Ultimately, this holistic business system is about developing people. Do workers know their role and responsibilities? Do they have clear instructions for doing the work? Do they understand what waste is and how to eliminate? Have they been trained? Do they have the tools and resources to succeed? If all of this happens, workers will not have to wait for a workshop to improve their job or tasks they perform. They are continuously looking for the next improvement.

Developing a culture of continuous improvement starts with developing people. It takes years. Although culture is influenced from both the top down and bottom up, it's built from the ground, through people *learning*. I have worked with thousands of people through countless workshops over the years. My observation is that it's rare when someone knows the organization's vision, mission, strategy, and values. Having a rough sense of these abstract values is without doubt good—but it's the elements of people development that contribute most to a culture of continuous improvement.

An experience where a company's mission did guide "on-the-ground" behavior was my first job with Johnson & Johnson in a strategic planning role. One thing that stands out from working there was "the Credo," a mission statement that guided decision-making. It's been over 30 years but I still remember this mission statement. It details responsibilities to customers, employees, communities, and shareholders: "We believe that our first responsibility is to the doctors, nurses, hospitals, mothers, and all others who use our products. Our products must always be of the highest quality. We must constantly strive to reduce the cost of these products. Our orders must be promptly and accurately filled. Our dealers must make a fair profit."

Every month I sat down with my boss for half an hour to talk about what we did in the previous month to support the mission of the business and what we were going to be doing in the next month. It was about my development. It was ground up. I was being given a guide for making decisions and I understood the importance of everyone working in the same direction.

I left Johnson & Johnson to attend graduate school. During this time, the Tylenol crisis occurred. Seven people died because of tampered Tylenol. I happened to be in a marketing class when we learned about it. I presented a real-time case study on how Johnson & Johnson was going to handle the crisis and the decisions made. It played out exactly as I predicted. Why? Because I clearly understood and internalized the Johnson & Johnson mission. I knew where they were going, and everybody was on the same page. Everyone had a guide to quickly make decisions and to act.

The journey toward process perfection is never ending, but it is precisely this continuous pursuit that drives lasting organizational excellence. As demonstrated throughout this chapter, the key to sustainable improvement lies not in sporadic initiatives but in establishing standardized work as a foundation and systematically building upon it. The insurance claims case study illustrated how bringing structure to chaos through standardization can lead to both better regulatory compliance and increased productivity.

The path to improvement requires a delicate balance: Standard work must be rigid enough to ensure consistency yet flexible enough to evolve with better methods. When workers follow standards while being empowered to suggest improvements, organizations create a powerful engine for continuous advancement. This is not about achieving an abstract notion of perfection, but rather about fostering an environment where every process can be questioned, tested, and refined.

True empowerment emerges not from complete autonomy, but from giving workers the tools, training, and clear guidelines they need to succeed—along with the ability to contribute to improving those very guidelines. This approach develops problem-solving capabilities throughout the organization while maintaining the structural integrity that prevents chaos.

This chapter's examination of waste categories provides a practical framework for improvement, while the discussion of organizational culture, particularly through the Johnson & Johnson example, shows how clear mission alignment can guide decision-making at all levels. When combined with systematic observation, standardization, and continuous refinement, these elements create a robust foundation for ongoing process improvement.

The ultimate goal is not just better processes, but better people: workers who understand their role, recognize waste, and possess both the skills and motivation to drive improvement. While perfection may remain forever out of reach, organizations that embrace these principles can create a sustainable culture of continuous improvement that brings them ever closer to that ideal.

Chapter 9

The System Works *Everywhere*

The beauty and elegance of this system is that when followed faithfully, it delivers enduring results *everywhere*.

The principles that form the basis of this holistic business system, like the core ideals of any dynamic approach to creating value, are inherently fungible—applicable to a broad array of situations. That is their essential appeal, and the source of their enduring power.

Negotiating the balance between applying them rigidly like a recipe and applying them situationally to serve the specific context is a talent that develops over time with practice. But sticking to the fundamental physics of the system, as it were, ensures robust and repeatable success.

I developed an appreciation of the universality of these principles through my experiences in over 50 transformations as a frontline worker, executive, investor, or consultant at Moffitt. Everywhere means:

- Large or small
- Discrete (finished goods made by assembling distinct, individual parts)
- Process (goods in bulk, like chemicals or beverages)
- Administration (like insurance, healthcare, government)
- Retail
- Any industry
- Any location

We've witnessed or applied a version of this system to a wide range of organizations in many countries, discovering through experience how they apply. Just to name a few, this includes General Electric, Kaman Aerospace, Sargent Lock, MattressFirm, Kydex, Joseph Abboud, Fairrington Transportation, CHG Healthcare, Bosch, Massachusetts General Hospital, Jordan's Furniture, EmployBridge, PolyOne, Louisville Bedding Company, Sleep Train, Nordyne, Ergotron, Nortek, Bilco, TechAir, Exactech, Intel, RGE, UTC, Serta Simmons, NAPA, AMPAC, Mt Baker, Continental, Captek, Crouse-Hinds, Paper Excellence, Aden & Anais, American Pacific, CertainTeed, Oldcastle, Lifetouch, Basin Holdings, Basin Material Handling, Precision Machining, Black Diamond, Wenzel, Velonex, Hudson Harvest, Riverview Landscapes, Talus Holdings, Cy's Linen Service, Main Street Auto, and more.

SIZE DOESN'T COUNT

We've learned a few key principles while documenting this system. For one, these principles apply regardless of the size of the organization or maturity (startup). Let's refer back to the company that made hockey socks.

This is where I learned that it was possible to create and implement a continuous improvement business system at a small company with fewer than 25 employees. The challenge was that we could not dedicate four to seven employees for a weeklong workshop and still meet customer requirements. We experimented with different schedules and found that if the team met for 90 minutes after lunch for two weeks, they were most effective. We followed the same workshop process as I had at previous companies, just spread out over 10 days.

We achieved a 48 percent increase in revenue and profits stemming from our improvements in quality, customer service, and productivity.

Over the last 15 years, two-thirds of my time was applied on improving processes that were not directly related to the manufacturing of a product. When most of the companies I was working with looked at their value stream analysis, they realized that the time to make the product or provide a service was a tiny fraction of the total time from order to cash. Therefore, improvement activities were focused on administrative and support processes.

The following are examples that were particularly impactful and hopefully will give a sense of how many improvements bring about transformational change.

I facilitated designing and implementing a continuous improvement system for laboratory animal science at a large hospital system. While research using animals is controversial, the application of their continuous improvement principles and resulting quality of care of the animals is undisputed. I learned firsthand how anytime work is done, such as feeding, cleaning cages, and ordering food and care supplies, there are opportunities to eliminate waste and improve safety, quality (of care and research), and productivity.

From the first workshop, I was amazed at how respectful the animal technicians were regarding the care and management of the animals. Combining this passion with the application of their continuous improvement system resulted in a breakthrough transformation. Our focus for one workshop was care for mice under a research protocol. The workshop team consisted of several animal technicians and a researcher.

We started by documenting the current state of cleaning the cages, feeding, and evaluating health. Wastes were identified, countermeasures tried, and standard work and visual management created. While difficult to determine if the care of the mice improved, the animal technicians praised how making their jobs a little easier, clarifying tasks, and having a way to ensure tasks were being completed gave them confidence that everything possible was being done to provide exceptional care and management.

Another workshop focused on nonhuman primates. I remember the first time I observed a monkey cage being washed. Poop was flying everywhere. This gave a new meaning to the term "eliminate waste." The team was able to reduce the time to clean a cage by 70 percent and ensure it was clean.

Certain types of problems crop up regardless of setting—such as the challenge of flow. At a regional hospital, the challenge was long waiting time in the emergency room. The workshop team observed and documented the current state. Watching the waste of waiting was tiresome. These were the waiting points in the emergency room for a patient with a broken arm:

- Patient arrives and waits to register.
- Patient waits for a room to be available.
- Patient waits to be seen by a doctor.
- Patient waits to be taken for any tests the doctor ordered.
- Patient waits to be tested.
- Patient waits to be brought back to room.
- Patient waits for the doctor to review test results and prescribe.
- Patient waits to get cast on arm.
- Patient waits to be discharged.

The only place without waiting was when the patient was asked to pay the bill. The countermeasure implemented in these types of emergencies was to have a triage nurse immediately send the patient for x-ray. When the doctor met the patient for the first time, they had the test results and could set the arm. This was a "one and done" for the doctor and eliminated much of the long wait times in the process. Total time was reduced by an average of three hours.

As this hospital continued to reduce waiting times across all emergencies, they put an electronic sign outside the hospital that showed the emergency room current wait time. For those who drove by the hospital regularly, confidence increased that if they had an emergency, this was the place to go. No matter the industry or process, customers expect product or services when they want or need them.

I learned how applying these principles can boost the quality and fast delivery of such low-tech yet process-intensive businesses as manufacturing men's suits (discussed earlier). Many years later this business continues to succeed and innovate.

A nonmanufacturer that has thrived with a holistic business system provides medical staffing on an interim basis. Over a three-year period, their implementation increased profits by 50 percent, reduced employee turnover by 24 percent, and reduced receivables (DSO) by 29 percent. This organization is repeatedly ranked in the "top ten best company to work for." The worth of the business has increased profoundly.

A workshop I facilitated at this medical staffing company with significant impact was focused on reducing licensing time for doctors in a new state. The team documented that the current time from request to issuance was 65 days. They processed over 100 requests per month. Actual time spent working on a request was less than eight hours. It is not uncommon for a process to have touch time less than 2 percent of total lead time. The team identified several bottlenecks in the process that caused waiting. Reducing these resulted in a 29 percent reduction in number of days to process.

LISTEN TO THE PEOPLE DOING THE WORK

Their reduction in employee turnover was partially the result of improvements identified from the voice of the customer workshop. VOC process is a structured approach to obtain unfiltered opinions. Typically, a customer is asked an open-ended question about a product or service. In this case the customers were the employees. The team asked more than 40 employees, "Tell us about working here." A typical first response was "What do you want to know?" The interviewer response was "Whatever comes to mind." Over 500 comments were written word for word, and were summarized based on how often and early in the interview the comments were made.

This was truly listening to the people who do the work. Many conclusions were reached and changes made. For example, it was amazing how important work schedule was. Some wanted to start early so they could catch kids after school; some wanted to start later to be able to manage morning activities at home. This led to flexible schedules and pioneering work-from-home options. Overall, turnover was reduced by more than 24 percent.

Another memorable experience of how a holistic business system could work in any company or organization was when we were asked by the owner of a private equity company—which was thriving with their system—to apply it to property management. They owned several luxury apartment complexes that the owner considered to be well run and profitable. However, because of success with holistic business systems across their portfolio, they wondered if similar magnitude of results could be achieved at the apartments.

There was no crisis to resolve, just a challenge to identify and implement improvements that would yield results not seen before in this industry. With this in mind, the workshop team started with a value stream analysis and improvement plan. The team mapped the current state of the tenant experience: first visit to the office, lease signing, move in, residence, maintenance, move out.

The team discovered that the typical time from a tenant moving out to a new tenant moving in was 30 days. As soon as the tenant moved out, they would inspect the apartment, determine what was needed, order parts/materials, and schedule necessary contractors. The actual work only took a few days—again, a typical result where the cycle time (touch time) was a fraction of the lead time (span time).

This led to a workshop focused on reducing the turnover time. After documenting the current process, a team member asked why they were not performing the inspection three to four weeks prior to move-out date. According to the lease they were able to perform the inspection as soon as the tenant notified management that they were not renewing their lease. With advanced inspection, they were able to order material and contractors to synchronize with tenant move-out. Wow, turnover dropped from three to four weeks to three to four days! New standard work was created to inspect ahead of time and order supplies and schedule contractors so the work could start the day after moving out. An additional month's rent for several hundred turnovers across multiple apartment complexes added up to hundreds of thousands in additional revenue per year. Solutions are usually the easy part and often obvious if you clearly understand the current condition.

Another workshop at the apartments conducted a voice of the customer (tenant). They asked an open-ended question: "Tell us about living at (property name)?" The top issue was how long it took to resolve "punch lists." These are the concerns a tenant has about needed repairs when they move in. Often the necessary supplies and fixtures were not readily available to resolve the tenant's issue. This led to a workshop creating a material replenishment system, or kanban, for parts to keep on hand in maintenance. For example, if you know the number of door handles you replace per month and how long it takes to order them, the order point and quantity can be determined for replenishment. Over time, tenant satisfaction scores improved 20–50 percent, depending on the property.

Another major discovery from the voice of the customer (tenant) was the importance of different amenities such as clubhouse, pool, workout room, dog park, and so on. The preconceived notion was that a clubhouse was very impor-tant to tenants. Unfiltered feedback from tenants said oth-erwise. This helped guide future capital expenditures and avoid building clubhouses. Interestingly, a dog park was a much higher want compared to a new or renovated club-house. Overall, applying their proven business system from their portfolio companies to property management exceeded expectations.

When working with a polymer manufacturer, I learned how applying these basic principles can transform a continuous flow "process" operation and have a corollary impact on key metrics such as safety. Raw materials go into one end of a series of machines and the finished product comes out at the end. Very little labor was required to make the product because the machines do most of the work.

When we walked in the building producing polymer, the facilitator shouted, "Stop, everyone back to the conference room." That was as far as we got in our first workshop, a value stream analysis and improvement plan, when we first entered the factory.

When we went to the workplace we saw powdery material everywhere: on the floor, on the walls, on the equipment, and in the air. For safety reasons we returned to the confer-ence room. My message was that this was the worst manu-facturing I had ever seen.

The focus of the workshop, which gradually evolved based on what we learned, and as a result of facts about current state being uncovered, changed to "What must happen to keep the raw materials in the machines?"

Based on this refocusing of purpose, the team made many repairs to the equipment during the workshop. Follow-up workshops put in place preventive maintenance (done by skilled maintenance technicians) and autonomous maintenance (cleaning, inspection, and lubrication done by the machine operators). Operators started to take care of their equipment like they took care of their cars. Over time they were able to keep the raw materials in the machines, which had a transformational impact on safety, quality, morale, and wasted raw materials.

Having worked with many continuous-flow processes (rocket fuel, cookies, ice cream, beer, drywall), I learned that total productive maintenance has had a big impact on quality, delivery, and cost structure. Instead of being insulted by the "worst manufacturing ever," the company took this as the rallying message for their continuous improvement journey.

The benefits of this approach spilled into other areas, one of which was triggered by failure mode and effects analysis (FMEA), something that was required by their largest customer. Traditional problem-solving focuses on something that has already happened. FMEA focuses on what could go wrong in the future and having countermeasures in place to prevent future problems.

Instilling a proactive mindset toward problems resulted in numerous insights that led to improvements. The team started by brainstorming what failures could happen in the future with process, product, or systems. For each failure mode they identified the severity of potential impact. They then assessed the likelihood or probability of each potential failure and how often it could occur.

A potential failure mode that was ranked with the highest severity and likelihood was if temperature in the factory rose over 100 degrees. The building was not air conditioned and had never experienced temperatures this high. If the temperature was over 100 degrees, it could severely impact the quality of the polymer that was being produced and clog the flow of material in the machines. With climate change, the likelihood of temperatures reaching this level was highly probable.

Countermeasures were put in place for all the potential failures with high risk. In this case the decision was made to have a plan to shut down the production line if temperatures reached a certain level, thereby avoiding the potential quality and downtime issues. For the customer it was not enough to quickly solve problems; they wanted to make sure that problems didn't occur in the first place.

The examples presented in this chapter demonstrate the remarkable versatility and universal applicability of the holistic business system. From manufacturing men's suits to managing laboratory animals, from polymer production to property management, the system's core principles have proven their worth across an extraordinarily diverse range of settings. What makes this possible is not just the flexibility of the system, but its grounding in fundamental principles that transcend industry boundaries.

The system's success in such varied contexts stems from its focus on universal challenges that every organization faces: reducing wait times, eliminating waste, improving quality, and creating value for customers. Whether applied to a small startup with 25 employees or a major healthcare institution, these principles remain constant. The key lies in understanding how to adapt the application while maintaining fidelity to the core concepts.

Perhaps most importantly, this chapter illustrates that the system's effectiveness isn't limited to traditional manufacturing environments where these principles originated. The same methodologies that improve factory floor operations can transform service operations, healthcare delivery, and property management. Even in cases where there was no obvious crisis to solve—such as the luxury apartment complexes—the systematic application of these principles unveiled substantial opportunities for improvement.

The lessons learned from failures are equally valuable. They remind us that while the system provides powerful tools for execution, it must be guided by clear-eyed analysis of market realities and customer needs. Success comes from combining the system's methodologies with unfiltered voice-of-customer feedback and fact-based decision-making.

As organizations continue to evolve and new industries emerge, the holistic business system proves its enduring relevance by addressing fundamental challenges that remain constant: the need to eliminate waste, reduce lead time, improve quality, and create value. Its power lies not in rigid prescriptions, but in providing a framework that can be thoughtfully adapted to any context while maintaining its essential principles.

Chapter 10

Align Around
Value, Relentlessly

"Why is it so hard to start at the right place, to correctly define value? Partly because most producers want to make what they are already making and partly because many customers only know how to ask for some variant of what they are already getting. They simply start in the wrong place and end up at the wrong destination. Then, when providers or customers do decide to rethink value, they often fall back on simple formulas—lower cost, increased product variety through customization, instant delivery—rather than jointly analyzing value and challenging old definitions to see what's really needed."

– Lean Thinking,
Jim Womack and Dan Jones

I once consulted for a company that warehoused books, who demonstrated how breaking free from current thinking can deliver radically new value when they reimagined how to deliver books. While other companies at the time were printing a large quantity of books on conventional printing presses and storing them in a warehouse, they took a fundamentally different approach.

What the customer wanted was a specific book delivered in a short period. They did not care if it was in the warehouse. The team identified new technology that could print one book at a time. No need for forecasting what titles and quantities to print, batch printing, and storage in the warehouse. No more out-of-stock situations or long delivery times. By rejecting the standard assumption that books had to be in stock, they created a whole new business model of printing what the customer ordered, when they wanted it, and delivering promptly.

The radical value came not only from identifying new technology but from a willingness to question century-old practices. They succeeded by temporarily suspending the model of "how things have always been done" and creating space for a genuine customer-centered solution that addressed problems most industry insiders had simply accepted as unavoidable. Ironically, print-on-demand has been cannibalized by electronic books. What customers value keeps changing.

What a customer values is a moving target that changes over time. What's important to a customer is inherently dynamic rather than static, evolving continuously through their experiences. We need to avoid the know-it-all attitude and continually strive to understand changing needs. Businesses that stay attentive to these evolving needs are better positioned to maintain customer loyalty and discover new opportunities for growth.

What's needed is a relentless drive to deliver value—now—despite the prevailing forces that stack up inside a business around the way things are being done. Processes entrench themselves within an organization through the force of inertia, creating resistance that undermines value creation. When established procedures become ingrained, they transform into unquestioned default behaviors that employees follow reflexively.

Value represents the True North of this system. All activity must be aligned around one shining priority: deliver value to the customer—when they want it, how they want it, where they want it. All improvement actively consists of relentlessly and thoroughly rethinking all transactions with the aim of eliminating everything that does *not* provide value, and then working from that starting point to deliver more value. Correctly defining value represents the fundamental starting point for any journey of improvement and excellence. Delivering value to the customer in turn delivers to employees and stakeholders.

Easier said than done. It's remarkable how much wasted activity creeps into daily work. Just as weeds tend to appear gradually and often go unnoticed, waste in work processes typically creeps in slowly. By the time you notice a significant problem, the "weeds" have already established roots in organizational practices.

Waste tends to infiltrate processes during times of change or when attention is focused elsewhere. A period of rapid growth in a company, for instance, might lead to hasty process additions that become permanent despite their inefficiency. A business that is losing money can slash costs and sacrifice quality and cause inefficiencies.

Prevention is easier than cure in both cases. Just as a gardener might use mulch to prevent weeds, organizations can develop people to be gardeners to see waste, eliminate it, and prevent it from recurring. A holistic business system is primarily about developing gardeners.

There's also a similarity in how both require ongoing maintenance. A garden is never permanently weeded, and organizational efficiency is never permanently achieved. Both require regular attention and "pruning" to maintain their health and productivity.

Perhaps most importantly, both weeds and waste can appear useful. Similarly, wasteful processes often survive because they seem to add value, like excessive meetings that feel productive but actually drain time and energy from real work. What starts as a focused meeting can evolve into a lengthy session with unnecessary participants and divergent discussions. People get added to keep them in the loop, agendas wander, and soon the original purpose is diluted.

At one company I led, I discovered that supervisors were spending almost half of their work week in meetings. *Half a week.* This was time that could have been used for developing everyone in their department. We got to this point because many managers did not know how to run an effective meeting and were trying to keep as many people as possible in the loop. There were no standards (leader standard work) in place for supervisors or managers.

A workshop team dug in. They were shocked how meetings had creeped over the years to comprise 50 percent of a supervisor's time. The team decided to keep the morning huddle meeting, and all other meetings for the week were canceled. The agenda for the 20-minute huddle looked like this: Review results from yesterday (5 min), plan for today (5 min), ask/discuss ideas to eliminate waste (5 min), safety moment (2 min). A one-hour block was put on the calendar every Friday for a communication meeting. If anyone at the company wanted to meet with the supervisors, they had to ask the manager to get on the agenda for this Friday meeting. To prevent meeting creep, only the department manager could schedule additional meetings for problem resolution. The agenda or standard work for a problem-solving meeting was to spend 90 percent of time on root cause analysis and the last 10 minutes on countermeasures or solutions. Amazing that when we got to the root cause, we rarely needed the full 10 percent of the time to determine the course of action.

The team freed up many hours in the week. They implemented standards to improve meeting effectiveness and avoid meeting creep. Freed-up time was reallocated to people development activities.

Another example of how waste can creep into daily work that most can empathize with is email. When I started my career, email was not widely used. Now employees and associates spend much of their time on it. An employee might start by checking email a few times daily but gradually develop a habit of constantly monitoring. Each peek and notification breaks their concentration. We all have probably received a mass email to provide information and, invariably, some recipients hit "reply all" and the multiplying effect starts. Everyone has probably also received an email at work that they should not have. This creep has even spilled into our personal lives.

I participated in many workshops focused on the waste email has created. Common countermeasures were to standardize and educate the organization: Do not routinely "reply all." Know when to send and when not to. Know when to visit and when to use the phone. Keep to a schedule for checking email. Use filters to weed out spam. At the company I am currently leading, we also have a "no emails on the weekend" policy. It is a constant effort. We make gains and waste creeps back in.

Authorization is another common waste of overprocessing. One inefficient process often spawns related inefficiencies. For example, a poorly designed approval process might lead to people creating workarounds, which then require additional oversight, generating even more bureaucracy. I have seen many situations where a barrier to keeping the work moving is an unnecessary approval.

A workshop team that was focused on the total time to receive a part from a supplier discovered this. The process was that the customer would order a part from an inside salesperson. The salesperson would send a request to the CEO to obtain the part from a supplier. After approval, the part would be ordered. When received, the part was sent out to the customer. The total time was 10–15 days. There was much expediting along the way. The perception was the supplier was slow. The reality was the supplier had the product in stock and was able to deliver in one day. The order was sitting in the CEO's inbox for many days. He was the bottleneck. He had put a process in place that every purchase order had to go through him. He did this because one time someone ordered something they should not have. The countermeasure was to set limits of authority for inside salespeople to purchase parts for customers and get the CEO only involved in high-dollar orders. Time to supply the customer was reduced to three to five days.

I have dozens of examples where a review or approval was put in place because of a problem. Eventually, the problem was resolved, yet the extra work was not removed.

Documentation can become another source of waste. Initially designed to capture essential information, documentation requirements often expand over time. Teams might begin recording excessive details "just in case," creating reports that no one fully reads, or maintaining outdated documents because "We've always done it this way." One month we had IT send only the reports that were clearly used. Many reports were held back to see if those on distribution noticed they were missing. Not surprisingly, we terminated many reports every quarter. Many times they were generated because of a problem. Although the problem was resolved, no one had gone back to stop the report, and the total number of reports crept up.

Information technology systems (IT) can be a contributor to waste creep. Companies might adopt new software to increase efficiency but end up creating parallel systems where they maintain both old and new methods. IT systems can also standardize waste. I have been involved with a few major ERP systems (enterprise resource planning). Unfortunately, work processes were not improved at first and we standardized waste. The systems way became the standard even if it was suboptimal, essentially standardizing waste. This caused countless problems and waste down the line.

A company I worked with held a workshop to improve work in process (inventory) accuracy. They had a new ERP system, and a module called Shop Floor Control. Every time material or a part moved through the production process, it was scanned into the computer system, and data such as quantity and location was entered. The theory was that the accountants and salespeople would be able to know where in the production process each part was and when it would be completed.

The reality was garbage in and garbage out. The information was unreliable, and we had added extra work for the workers. The team realized they were trying to keep track of a wasteful process. Start to finish was a few weeks. If we went from raw material to finished goods in a few days, we would not need to keep track of work in process. We ended up turning off Shop Floor Control and focusing on reducing the throughput time, from raw material to finished good. We had used a system to standardize waste and, in the process, created even more waste.

Unfortunately, our lack of understanding of customer requirements can lead us astray. My leadership in the local economic development organizations led Hillary Clinton (who was senator of New York at the time) to approach us regarding manufacturing for a startup in the security field.

The company designed a machine that would clean and sterilize mail. This was during the anthrax scare, and there were several letters with white substances around the country. The US government and many major corporations were pushing for delivery of this sterilizer. The size and complexity of the sterilizing machine were similar to the machines we produced for the textile industry, so this was a good fit.

Our business system guided us to quickly set up world-class manufacturing. We had it all: good flow, quality at the source, excellent workplace organization, standard work, visual management everywhere, and more. We built the first units for the United Nations, and our confidence in manufacturing and expected profits were off the charts.

We desperately wanted this to be successful. This was the company's big break. Innovative technology, market demand, great manufacturing capabilities: This was a grand slam. The result of this project? It failed.

The red flags were obvious. We heard only what we wanted to hear and selected the data that supported a grand slam. Each sterilizer cost around $60,000. We thought that oh, yeah, the demand is there. But the potential buyers had real reservations about the efficacy of the equipment, the cost, and their ability to use it. The anthrax crisis had ended. But we just focused on the information that fit our belief that this could be a huge, profitable project. We cherry-picked the information that supported our hope that it was going to work, and people were going to buy it. That did not happen.

Whether it's a workshop, innovation, or startup, improvement activities need to be fact-based and careful not to succumb to confirmation bias. Learning unfiltered what the customer requires is critical to staying on the road. Happily, the production of textile machines continues to thrive.

Fortunately, during the COVID crisis we avoided this mistake. I led a startup to produce surgical masks and half-mask respirators. We partnered with a major producer of fuel products. Their chemical division produces the ingredients for filter material and had mask design capabilities. We had manufacturing and distribution capabilities, and our known business system set us apart as a partner. At the time, there was a severe shortage of masks. This was an opportunity to help society.

The facts, however, dictated otherwise. A close examination of the international supply chain showed the country was about to be flooded with masks. We shut down the project before overproduction could occur.

It's vital to remember always that value is created by providing what is important to employees, customers, and stakeholders. Here are examples of how eliminating waste creates value:

Eliminate Overproduction:

- *Employees* benefit from reduced stress and clearer priorities because they're focused on immediate customer needs rather than building what may not be needed now.
- *Customers* receive products more quickly because resources aren't tied up making unneeded items.
- *Stakeholders* see improved cash flow and reduced storage/carrying costs.

Eliminate Waiting:

- *Employees* stay engaged and productive, leading to higher job satisfaction.
- *Customers* experience faster service and shorter lead times.
- *Stakeholders* benefit from improved operational efficiency and labor utilization.

Eliminate Transportation:

- *Employees* spend more time on value-adding activities.
- *Customers* receive products faster due to streamlined logistics.
- *Stakeholders* see reduced transportation costs and lower risk of damage during movement.

Eliminate Over-Processing:

- *Employees* can focus on meaningful work rather than on unnecessary steps.
- *Customers* don't pay for non-value-added activities.
- *Stakeholders* benefit from improved productivity and reduced costs.

Eliminate Inventories:

- *Employees* do not have to search.
- *Customers* receive products on time with higher quality and less risk of obsolescence.
- *Stakeholders* see reduced working capital tied up in inventory and storage costs.

Eliminate Moving:

- *Employees* experience improved safety, less physical strain and fatigue from unnecessary movement.
- *Customers* benefit from faster service as employees work more efficiently.
- *Stakeholders* see improved productivity and reduced risk of workplace injuries.

Eliminate Defects:

- *Employees* feel more pride in their work and spend less time on rework.
- *Customers* receive higher-quality products and better overall experience.
- *Stakeholders* benefit from reduced warranty costs and stronger brand reputation.

VOICE OF THE CUSTOMER METHODOLOGY

Correctly defining value represents the starting point for any journey of improvement and excellence. It requires learning what is important to employees, customers, and stakeholders. One way is utilizing Voice of the Customer methodology.

Voice of the Customer methodology may be used any time we want to understand what's important to customers or employees.

- A system for translating unfiltered requirements into appropriate action plans and product development.
- A system that emphasizes staying focused on what is important to employees, customers, and stakeholders.
- A standardized approach to document and keep track of their needs, so everyone in the company buys in and understands them.
- A technique to help "neutralize the voice of the know-it-alls."
- A planning methodology that organizes relevant information that helps us make better decisions.

I led the introduction of a holistic business system at a manufacturer of air conditioning equipment. We quickly reversed the trend of declining profits through top-line growth, productivity, and process improvements. Key to this turnaround was better understanding customer needs, or Voice of the Customer.

A workshop team was tasked with better understanding what is important to the customer regarding water source heat pumps, which refers to a heating and cooling system that transfers heat between a building and a water source. In heating mode, it extracts heat from water and transfers it into the building; in cooling mode, it removes heat from the building and releases it into the water.

The team started by asking 45 customers to tell us about their experiences with the water source heat pumps. That's it, a straightforward, open-ended question. We didn't lead them in one direction or another. We didn't show our biases. We wanted to understand what was at the top of their mind. The customers sometimes said, "Well, what do you want to know?" Our response was always "Whatever comes to mind." We wrote down exactly what each person said on one piece of paper and read it back to them, asking them to confirm. The team continued to write down one thought per sheet of paper until the customers were done speaking. When they'd run out of things to say we thanked them, and the call was over. We did not problem-solve on the call, only listened.

The team then created a matrix reflecting how early and often a comment was made. The assumption going into the kaizen was that price was going to be the most important issue. The team learned the customers' number one concern was getting replacement units. Price was not even in the top five.

The initial order was usually a large shipment for an entire building. We had many months' advanced notice to produce the order. However, if a unit had to be replaced, the customer would try to order a single replacement unit. They needed these replacement units that day, not in days or weeks or months. The company was set up for large build-to-order for new construction, and the long production lines were not able to produce single units. If we could not ship the same day, the customer would go to our competition.

To address this, the team created a small cell that could quickly produce any size unit in small quantities. The operator would look in the morning to see what was ordered yesterday (pull) and that's what they would build that day (one-piece flow). This was a breakthrough for meeting customer requirements and transforming into cellular manufacturing.

The team asked our coach, "Why didn't we just send out a survey?" We learned that the questions you ask can bias the answers. If the team had asked the customer whether price was important, the customer would say yes. Asking open-ended questions and getting unfiltered feedback on what the customers want led the team in the direction of delivering replacement units within a day, as opposed to weeks or months to meet the needs of our customers.

Additional teams used Voice of the Customer to understand not only the customer's needs for all the other product lines but also to better understand what was important to our employees.

A workshop team asked employees what it was like to work for the company. A top issue emerged that if they were out a few hours for an appointment they would get charged for a full day off. The team changed the policy, resulting in improvement in both morale and retention.

Another issue was lack of flexibility with shift start times. Many employees had family needs early in the morning or after school. The historical thinking was "How can we possibly have people start at different times and productively run a manufacturing cell?" The company held a workshop to figure out how to manage with different start times and number of days worked per week, created standard work to support the changes, and offered flexibility and choice to our employees. This, too, resulted in improved morale and retention.

As we've explored throughout this chapter, aligning around value is not just a business strategy; it's a fundamental mindset shift that transforms how organizations operate. The relentless pursuit of value requires vigilance, curiosity, and the courage to question entrenched practices that no longer serve customers, employees, or stakeholders.

The examples we've examined—from print-on-demand book publishing to streamlining meetings and approval processes—all highlight a critical truth: What constitutes value is constantly evolving. Yesterday's innovative solution can quickly become tomorrow's obsolete process. This dynamic reality demands that we approach our work with humility, regularly suspending our assumptions about "how things have always been done" to create space for genuine customer-centered solutions.

Perhaps most challenging is the recognition that waste, like weeds in a garden, will continually attempt to creep back into our processes. Meetings expand beyond their useful purpose, emails multiply unnecessarily, approval chains grow longer, and documentation becomes excessive. The organization that thrives is one that develops "gardeners"—people at all levels who can identify waste, eliminate it, and prevent its return.

The Voice of the Customer methodology demonstrated how easy it is to misunderstand what truly matters to those we serve. When we approach customers with genuine curiosity rather than preconceived notions, we often discover that their priorities differ dramatically from our assumptions. Similarly, when we listen openly to employees, we find opportunities to create value that might otherwise remain hidden.

Ultimately, aligning around value means creating a system where the True North guides all activity: delivering value to customers when they want it, how they want it, and where they want it. This alignment, in turn, creates value for employees through more meaningful work and for stakeholders through sustainable business performance.

The journey of improvement and excellence begins with correctly defining value, a simple concept that proves remarkably difficult in practice. It requires us to jointly analyze and challenge old definitions with our customers, moving beyond simple formulas to discover what's truly needed. When we commit to this path of relentless value creation, we don't just improve processes; we transform our entire approach to business.

Chapter 11

Putting It All Together

Implementing a holistic continuous improvement system delivers profound benefits across an organization. Strategically, it provides a competitive edge through enhanced adaptability to market changes and customer demands, while systematically reducing costs and elevating quality and on-time delivery to new heights. Operationally, processes become increasingly optimized as workflows grow more efficient and problems are addressed before they become critical issues.

This approach ensures better resource utilization and enables more informed decision-making based on data from improvement cycles. The impact on people and culture cannot be overstated—employee engagement flourishes as staff become active participants in workplace enhancement, while knowledge sharing across functions accelerates organizational learning. An innovation culture naturally emerges when small improvements are constantly encouraged, and seeing positive changes implemented significantly boosts morale throughout the organization.

The long-term sustainability benefits are equally compelling. Organizations develop greater resilience against disruptions, create scalable processes that accommodate growth without proportional resource increases, build customer loyalty through consistently exceeding expectations, and often reduce their environmental impact through efficiency gains. Together, these advantages create a self-reinforcing cycle of excellence that drives ongoing organizational success.

Implementing this business system begins with establishing strong leadership commitment, where executives sponsor the initiative, align improvement goals with strategic objectives, and allocate necessary resources and budget. This foundation is strengthened by defining your improvement philosophy, developing a governance structure, setting clear roles and responsibilities, and establishing baseline metrics to measure future progress. Building organizational capability follows, through training employees in improvement methodologies, developing internal coaches and champions, and creating a common language and approach that everyone understands.

The system design phase involves selecting appropriate principles and fundamentals: establishing standard problem-solving approaches, creating mechanisms for idea submission and implementation, and developing management systems for accountability. All the breakthrough transformations I have been involved with resulted from companies developing their own system drawing from a huge body of work around operational excellence and continuous improvement.

Initial workshops should then be implemented to target high-impact, visible improvement opportunities, apply improvement methodologies to achieve rapid wins, and document and share successes throughout the organization. Supporting infrastructure must be developed, including knowledge management systems, regular review mechanisms, recognition and reward programs, and robust tracking and reporting systems. As momentum builds, successful practices can be scaled across departments, improvement processes standardized, and improvement activities integrated into daily work. Finally, the system must be sustained and evolve by regularly assessing effectiveness, refining approaches based on lessons learned, evolving the system as organizational needs change, and connecting improvement efforts to concrete business results.

PUTTING IT ALL TOGETHER AT A GLOBAL HOLDING COMPANY

In 2018 I was hired as chief operating officer at a global holding company to create and implement an operational excellence business system. I also had management responsibilities for four out of eight business units, corporate human resources, and information technology. Over a five-year period, this company generated a more than 500 percent increase in enterprise value.

This company consisted of eight diverse business units at the time. In the energy sector we had rental pipe, downhole tools, consumables supply, well completion, power supply, and inspection services. In the industrial sector we had precision machining, packaging, and material handling.

The journey started with a new board member who was the principal at a major private equity company. His firm achieved many breakthrough transformations by implementing continuous improvement business systems. I was fortunate to have consulted with many of the portfolio companies and I knew this new board member well. As a board member of this global holding company, he brought his knowledge and passion regarding improvement initiatives to the board of directors and the CEO, thereby establishing strong leadership commitment to start a continuous improvement journey. Leadership commitment was the start.

The next step was to build organizational capability. I remember I was facilitating a workshop in Canada that was focused on manufacturing drywall compound when I received a call from the board member asking if I would meet with the global holding company CEO to discuss joining the company. My first meeting with the CEO was on the factory floor of the business unit that provided material handling solutions. It was a mess and losing money. The bridge was burning. Although the CEO had little experience with any of the continuous improvement models, I was encouraged that for our introductory meeting we went to the workplace and observed the work being done. We quickly aligned on the opportunities in front of us and started discussing who could be dedicated to the operational excellence office and what was needed to get started. I had not yet accepted the job, and we were already designing and planning a new business system. I soon joined as chief operating officer and lined up resources from Moffitt Consulting, the company that had supported the board members over many years. This was the start of building organizational capability and executive leadership.

The company faced a series of challenges across its many operating units in the United States, Canada, and Mexico. These challenges encompassed the need to improve quality, on-time delivery, service, and cost structure. The challenges underscored the need to adopt a systematic approach to operational improvement, laying the groundwork for the collaborative endeavor with Moffitt to develop and implement an operational excellence business system.

Developing the business system started with guidance from the board of directors and sharing what I learned from many turnarounds and transformations. Designing the system is a never-ending process because it too can be continuously improved. Back and forth communication between the board, executive team, presidents, and newly formed operational excellence team started to build the system.

All the company presidents were brought together at one factory for president's workshops. We had five teams rolling up their sleeves to learn by doing, make process improvements, and recommend refinements to the system. Concurrently, training meetings were held across the business units to introduce the system.

This business system embodies a holistic management approach focused on developing staff and operational excellence. It strategically targets waste reduction through value stream analysis, daily improvement efforts, and workshops. It implements fundamental principles while ensuring workplace organization and accountability and sets clear targets, driving the organization toward sustained improvement and success. It is focused on people, process, and principles (Figure 11.1).

Implementation started with identifying high-impact improvement opportunities. Every business unit held

Figure 11.1   The business system.

workshops to analyze their value streams and create improvement plans. Each business unit identified 50 to 80 improvement opportunities. Multiply by eight business units and at the start we had identified over 500 opportunities for improvement. They were prioritized based on impact on quality, delivery, service, and cost. The value stream analysis and improvement planning were repeated annually.

Not all opportunities required a workshop. If the problem and root cause were obvious and the countermeasure not controversial, we would just do it. Workshops were held when dealing with complex, cross-functional problems where the solution wasn't immediately obvious, requiring structured analysis, multiple perspectives, and dedicated time for improvements. These formal workshops, typically lasting three to four days, were ideal when team alignment was crucial, when data collection was necessary to understand root causes, or when the change affects multiple processes or departments. We use the same methodology for workshops or just do it (Figure 11.2).

Over five years Basin completed more than 400 workshops. Every location was required to conduct at least one workshop per month. Initially, most workshops were facilitated by Moffitt consultants. Over time, dedicated business system leaders developed facilitation skills, and workshops were increasingly facilitated internally. Workshops followed a rigorous format: observe, listen, identify waste, brainstorm, try, reflect, standard work, report.

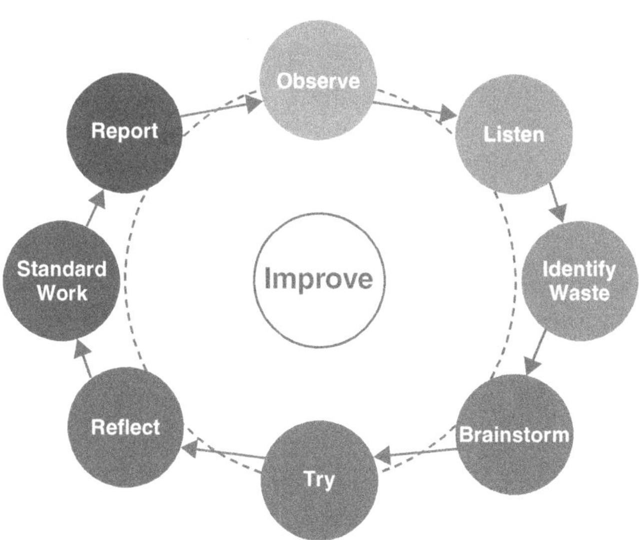

Figure 11.2 Workshop methodology.

OPERATING-LEVEL PERFORMANCE

Here are a few examples of workshops at one business unit:

- Weld line safety and flow: Reduced movement on the line by 50 percent; decreased labor hours per rack from 7.7 to 4.6; increased 5S score from 2.7 to 3.8; reduced quality rejects by 65 percent; identified and solved four safety issues

- Reduced forklifts: Developed manual conveyance and improved flow; 20k reduction in maintenance cost yearly; freed up one full-time team member to be relocated in the value stream; reduced safety risks associated with the operation of forklifts; reduced the chance of missing parts, due to increased visibility

- Weld line setup: Reduced weld work hours per rack from 2.6 to 1.8; reduced transportation by 146 ft per rack; estimated 925 hours back to the overall project; created 39 visual management tools; gained $22,200 through labor efficiency

- Fixture storage and tracking: Created a fixture storage process; sorted and removed 40 yards of waste from the yard; removed a total 16 tons of scrap from the yard; created standard work to ensure we sustain the fixture storage process; created one visual management tool

- Assembly flow: Established a plan for one-piece flow in the assembly area, supported by standard work procedures; 24,000 steps saved during the production process; reduced actual labor by 3.32 hours per rack; created five standard work instructions for the assembly process; saved 664 assembly labor hours over the course of the remainder of the run; corrected eight safety concerns

- Paint flow: Identified and corrected 19 safety concerns; created process to support one-piece flow; heating system put into place to keep the painters and paint warm in the winter; 100 percent reduction in downtime waiting on a forklift; air makeup system installed, allowing proper ventilation; high-speed door installed, allowing dry-room fans to function without disrupting air flow in the paint booths; tilter installed to tilt racks, allowing for the painters to easily paint the underside of racks; reduced transportation by an estimated 70 percent; estimated annual labor savings = $149,760

- Saw fabrication: Improved flow; reduced steps by 25 percent; reduced labor by 15 percent; increased in-house cut-to-length tube efforts by 60 percent

- Weld: Improved flow; increased weld capacity by 20 percent; reduced movement by 1500 feet per day; improved quality by allowing welders to focus on one weldment at a time; freed up 1,875 square feet and used the space to create five weld cells

- Fabrication and laser layout: Restored in-house fabrication; reduced outsourcing by 60 percent

- Aluminum welding: Developed a fully capable aluminum weld line; repurposed 960 square feet of underutilized space

At one of the business units, enhancing quality, delivery, service, and cost structure yielded a remarkable 20 percent increase in gross margin, equating to a $25 million boost in EBITDA (earnings before interest, taxes, depreciation, and amortization), alongside maintaining a flawless 100 percent on-time delivery record. Sales surged by 80 percent and the number of OSHA safety recordable incidents was reduced by 88 percent. Figure 11.3 provides a snapshot of their journey.

After the first year, all business started strategy deployment. This aligned our key objectives with day-to-day operations across all levels of the business. It began with leadership

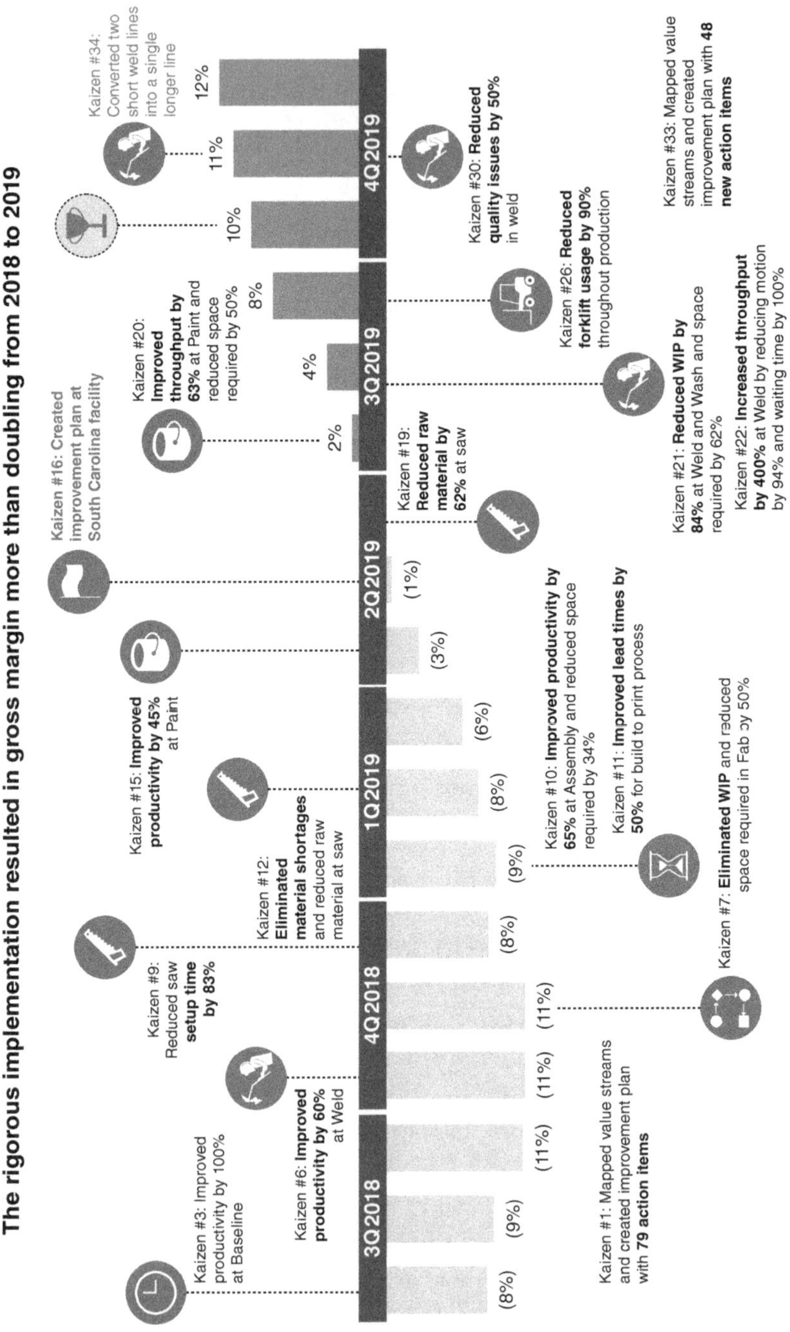

Figure 11.3   Snapshot of one business unit's journey.

establishing clear strategic priorities and measurable goals, which were then cascaded throughout the organization in a structured manner, ensuring every department and individual understands how their work contributes to the broader vision. The power of strategy deployment lies in its ability to create organizational coherence by connecting strategic planning with tactical execution, transforming abstract objectives into concrete actions while preventing the common disconnect between leadership aspirations and frontline activities.

We implemented this systematic approach because it dramatically improves focus by eliminating competing priorities, enhances accountability through transparent metrics and regular review cycles, fosters cross-functional collaboration to address complex challenges, and ultimately increases the probability of successful strategy execution. Unlike traditional top-down planning methods, strategy deployment encourages two-way communication through catchball processes where plans are refined based on feedback from those who will implement them, creating widespread ownership and commitment while ensuring that daily improvement activities remain perfectly aligned with the organization's most critical priorities, thereby maximizing the impact of continuous improvement efforts. It took us several annual cycles to get reasonably effective.

Throughout implementation, employee development was always at the forefront. Workshops were a great opportunity to learn from experience. We also held classroom training for the overall business system and specific principles. As part of their onboarding, new employees would attend an intro to the business system. If a workshop was going to be utilizing a specific tool, the participants would get training beforehand regarding that tool. Periodically, a three-day business system boot camp was held where operational excellence leaders from the business units would come together to share their experiences and learn from each other.

MAKING IMPROVEMENTS PART OF DAILY WORK

Over time, we gradually saw making improvements become part of everyday work rather than a separate activity, with everyone consistently asking, "How can we make this better?" and employees empowered to implement changes within their areas of responsibility. We got to the point in many areas where workers did not have to wait for a workshop to make an improvement or eliminate waste.

Through targeted initiatives and rigorous performance metrics, this global holding company and Moffitt embarked on a journey to address the challenges head-on, driving tangible results and unlocking new levels of operational excellence within the organization. Key performance indicators at the corporate level were safety, quality, on-time delivery, productivity (sales per total labor cost), and cost structure (variable margin).

Productivity, measured by sales per total labor cost, increased nearly 200 percent (Figure 11.4). This measurement holds significant importance, encompassing both production and SG&A (selling, general, administrative) labor. We believe if a company has industry-leading quality, delivery, service, and cost structure, they should grow revenue, gain market share, maximize price increases, and do it all more efficiently. With this principle in mind, we embarked on a journey to eliminate waste across diverse operating units, aiming to drive revenue growth, secure market share,

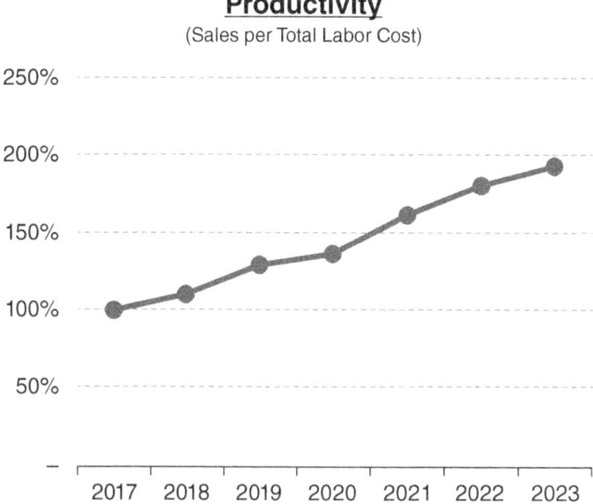

Figure 11.4   Productivity (sales per total labor cost).

optimize pricing, and enhance overall operational efficiency. Central to this effort was a focus on improving the sales per total labor cost metric, aligning with our belief in translating quality, delivery, and efficiency into tangible productivity enhancements.

It is remarkable that this measurement improved significantly during a period of substantial wage increases. We believed that paying people well was not just adding cost to the business but was a priceless investment.

Inventory turns increased by more than 100 percent (Figure 11.5). Over $45 million in "sleeping cash" was freed and redeployed into growth and acquisition initiatives. On-time delivery soared to world class levels.

Reducing inventory was not the goal; inventory was seen as a measurement of waste and poor flow. In addition, forecasts were often wrong because of rapidly changing customer

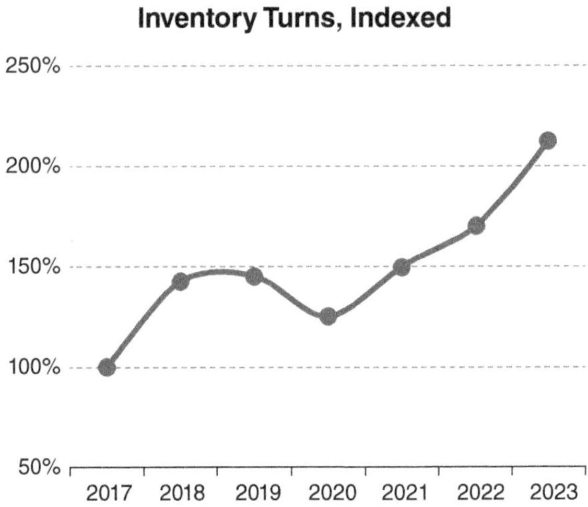

Figure 11.5   Inventory turns.

requirements. Improving flow, throughput time, and relentless elimination of waste achieved breakthrough customer service levels and cash.

Frequency of injuries declined by 60 percent (Figure 11.6). Every workshop includes a safety focus. Typically, the team may identify and resolve 5–10 safety issues during the workshop. Multiplying this by several hundred workshops, and thousands of safety issues have been resolved since implementation of the business system. In addition, workshop teams are trained to focus on identifying behavioral safety issues such as improper lifting or wearing personal protective equipment. Ensuring the safety of the workforce remained a paramount concern. While pursuing operational improvements, everyone committed to maintaining and even enhancing safety standards. The challenge lay in fostering a culture of continuous improvement without compromising on safety, because any gains in productivity were nonnegotiable if they came at the expense of employee well-being.

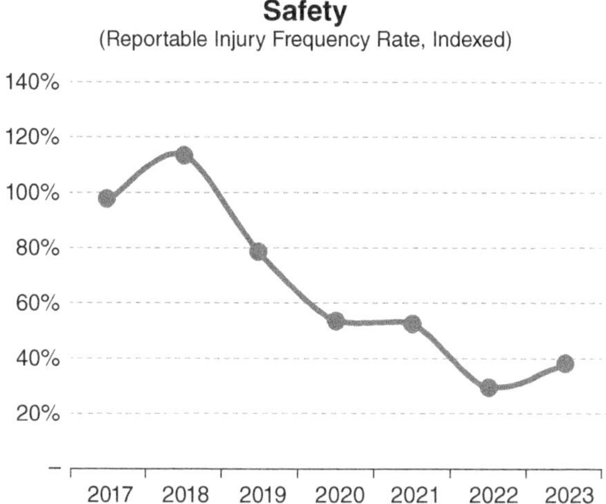

Figure 11.6   Safety.

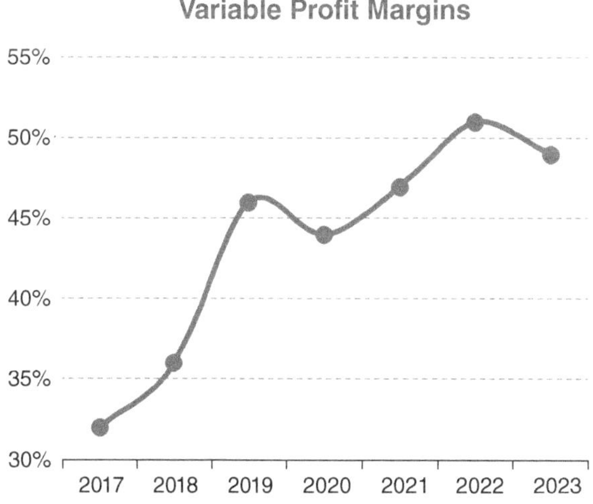

Figure 11.7   Variable profit margins.

Variable profit margins increased by 20 percent (Figure 11.7), which represents nearly $50 million to the bottom line. Again, this was accomplished by relentlessly eliminating waste.

THE CUSTOMER EXPERIENCE IS THE ULTIMATE KPI

The ultimate KPI (key performance indicator) is what the customer experiences. Exceptional performance has been recognized by being awarded Toyota Supplier of the Year for many years (Figure 11.8). This is the greatest recognition and indication of success for implementation of the business system.

In collaboration with Moffitt consultants, we developed a business system based on people development, empowering all employees and delivering best in class quality, delivery, service, and cost. This global holding company's journey demonstrates the transformative power of a well-implemented continuous improvement system. Over five years, this comprehensive approach delivered extraordinary results: a 500 percent increase in enterprise value; 20 percent higher profit margins, adding $50 million to the bottom line; 100 percent improvement in inventory turns, freeing $45 million in capital; and an 80 percent sales surge at one

Figure 11.8   Ultimate validation of business system.

business unit while maintaining perfect on-time delivery. Safety improved dramatically, with a 60 percent reduction in injuries, while productivity nearly tripled despite significant wage increases.

These achievements weren't accidental but resulted from methodical implementation: securing leadership commitment from the board level down, building organizational capability through targeted training and workshops, designing a customized business system, and implementing improvements across all business units. The company conducted over 400 workshops, addressing hundreds of high-impact opportunities, making improvement part of everyday work rather than a separate activity.

Perhaps most telling was the recognition from customers, with Toyota Supplier of the Year awards validating the company's excellence in quality, delivery, service, and cost. This case study proves that continuous improvement, when integrated as a holistic business system, creates a self-reinforcing cycle of excellence that benefits every stakeholder—customers receive better products and service, employees enjoy safer workplaces and higher wages, and shareholders see substantial returns on investment.

The journey was neither quick nor easy, requiring persistent effort in strategy deployment, employee development, and leadership commitment. But the results speak for themselves: a company transformed not just financially, but culturally—where waste elimination, problem-solving, and improvement became embedded in the organization's DNA. This comprehensive approach to operational excellence provides a blueprint for any organization seeking to achieve breakthrough performance in today's competitive business environment.

Chapter 12

The Sustaining Way of Creating Value

Throughout this book, we've explored a holistic approach to creating value—not just for owners, but for employees, customers, and society at large. This approach consistently produces superior results across industries, from manufacturing to healthcare, from technology to property management. The question that remains is not whether the system works—the evidence over decades conclusively shows that it does—but whether organizations will learn from it and develop a system that works for them.

The journey began with that pivotal moment at Crouse-Hinds, when a machine operator spoke up and suggested moving equipment a mere six inches. That single instance embodied what would become the cornerstone of this philosophy: being present, observing the work being done, and listening to the people who do the work. This seemingly small act of listening and responding to someone on the factory floor transformed not just the physical layout of equipment but the entire culture of the organization. It demonstrated that wisdom doesn't flow only from the top down but emerges from all levels when people are genuinely respected and heard.

The holistic business system examined in these pages encompasses far more than a set of tools or techniques. It represents a comprehensive framework built on foundational principles that reinforce each other. At its core is a management philosophy that values presence, direct observation, and active listening—practices that are increasingly rare in an age of remote management and digital dashboards. Leaders who commit to being physically present where the work happens gain insights that can never be captured in spreadsheets or status reports. The texture, rhythm, dignity, and reality of work are revealed only through direct engagement with processes and the people who perform them.

Strategy deployment translates this hands-on approach into organizational alignment. As seen in case after case, when organizations clearly articulate their objectives and engage in "catchball" between levels, they create not just alignment but ownership. Every person understands not only what needs to be accomplished but why it matters and how their specific contributions connect to the larger purpose. This thread of meaning runs through the organization, weaving individual efforts into collective achievement.

Value stream analysis provides the detailed roadmap for improvement, revealing what truly happens in the intricate flow of materials, information, and activities that comprise any process. When teams map their current state with honesty and precision, they often discover that the time spent actually adding value represents a tiny fraction of total lead time. This revelation—that most activities contribute little or nothing to what customers value—becomes the catalyst for transformation. The waste becomes visible, and once visible, it cannot be ignored.

Workshops drive immediate, tangible changes based on these insights. Unlike traditional improvement approaches that separate planning from execution, these intensive events compress the cycle of observation, analysis, experimentation, and implementation into days rather than months. The bias for action—for making changes now rather than waiting for perfect solutions—unleashes creativity and builds momentum. A 50 percent improvement implemented today creates more value than a theoretical 100 percent improvement that never materializes.

The fundamental principles explored in this book—takt time, one-piece flow, pull systems, setup reduction, total productive maintenance, workplace organization (5S), and voice of the customer, provide the technical foundation for operational excellence. These concepts, refined over decades of practice across many organizations, offer proven approaches to eliminating waste and creating flow. But they are not rigid formulas to be blindly applied. They are principles to be understood, adapted, and applied with intelligence to each unique situation.

Management systems sustain these gains through standard work, visual control, and leader standard work. Without disciplined approaches to maintaining improvements, organizations inevitably drift back toward old patterns and problems. Standard work creates a baseline for future improvement, visual controls make problems immediately apparent, and leader standard work ensures that managers fulfill their primary responsibility—developing the capabilities of their people.

A deep respect for people serves as both the moral foundation and the practical necessity of this system. Organizations that view employees primarily as costs to be minimized inevitably undermine their own potential. Those that respect workers as problem-solvers and value creators tap into an inexhaustible source of improvement. Throughout this book, numerous examples have shown how frontline workers, when properly supported and genuinely respected, identify opportunities that would never be visible from the executive suite.

A relentless focus on quality at the source transforms how organizations approach excellence. Rather than relying on inspection to catch defects after they occur, this approach builds quality into every step of the process. The contrast between the two automobile manufacturers described earlier—one staging vehicles for post-production repair, the other building quality in from the start—illustrates the profound difference in both effectiveness and philosophy. Building it right the first time isn't just more efficient; it's also more respectful of both workers and customers.

Learning emerges as the fundamental engine of continuous improvement. Organizations that view problems as opportunities for deeper understanding rather than occasions for blame create environments where people grow alongside their processes. The stories shared demonstrate how learning by doing, especially when guided by experienced mentors, develops capabilities far more effectively than classroom training alone. The focus shifts from knowing to understanding, from compliance to creativity.

The compounding power of small, consistent improvements transforms organizations over time. Like compound interest in finance, improvements build upon each other in ways that produce exponential rather than linear growth. A single setup reduction might save minutes; hundreds of such improvements across thousands of operations transform the entire rhythm and capability of an organization. The "base hits" accumulate into grand slams that competitors cannot match through episodic big-swing initiatives.

A commitment to perfecting processes through constant refinement acknowledges that excellence is never finished. The goal is not to reach a static endpoint but to create dynamic processes that continuously evolve toward ever-higher levels of performance. This mindset turns standard work from a constraint into a platform for innovation, where each iteration becomes the foundation for the next improvement.

An unwavering alignment around customer value keeps this entire system focused on what truly matters. Without this clarity about the ultimate purpose—creating what customers genuinely value—improvement activities can become disconnected from business outcomes. The voice of the customer methodology ensures that organizations ground their efforts in authentic understanding rather than assumptions about what matters most to those they serve.

Versions of this holistic business system have created billions in value across diverse industries and organizations, transforming not just balance sheets but the very culture of work itself. From the family-owned door manufacturer to the multinational energy enterprise, from the textile mill to the insurance company, this approach unleashes potential that traditional management methods leave dormant.

Today, too many organizations choose a different path—one focused on extracting value rather than creating it. This approach seeks ways to leverage capital to maximize short-term returns; hold customers captive through technical advantage or monopolistic positioning; treat employees as disposable costs rather than valuable assets; cut corners on quality, delivery, and service to meet quarterly targets; and celebrate financial engineering over operational excellence. The evidence of this approach appears in declining customer satisfaction and employee disengagement, all sacrificed for make-the-month profits.

The results of this value-extraction approach are predictable: fleeting financial gains followed by long-term decline, disengaged employees, dissatisfied customers, and diminished societal impact. The private equity model that focuses exclusively on financial restructuring rather than operational excellence exemplifies this approach. It may create wealth for a small group of investors, but it rarely builds enduring enterprises that serve all stakeholders.

The stark difference between these approaches is not just philosophical; it's practical. Organizations that embrace a holistic business system consistently outperform those that do not, especially over extended periods. They weather economic downturns more effectively, retain talent more successfully, and create more sustainable value for all stakeholders. The contrast becomes especially apparent during crises, when the resilience built through continuous improvement becomes a decisive advantage.

Organizations considering implementing this holistic business system should remember that the journey begins with a clear-eyed assessment of the current state. Mapping value streams, identifying waste, and listening—really listening—to customers and employees provides essential information. The unfiltered truth about present conditions, however uncomfortable, provides the only solid foundation for improvement. Organizations that begin with defensive justifications of the status quo rarely progress beyond incremental adjustments to existing systems.

Leaders must commit to being present where the work happens. There is no substitute for going to the workplace, observing the work being done, and listening to those who do it. No report, dashboard, or presentation can replace this direct experience. Leaders who spend their days in conference rooms reviewing PowerPoint slides about operations rather than witnessing them firsthand inevitably make decisions based on filtered, sanitized versions of reality. The wisdom required for transformation emerges from direct engagement, not delegated observation.

Each organization must build its own system that respects its unique circumstances while challenging its assumptions. While the principles explored in this book are universal, implementation must be tailored to specific contexts. A hospital will not implement these ideas exactly as a manufacturing plant does, nor should it. The art of adaptation requires deep understanding of both the principles and the setting where they'll be applied. This is why mechanical imitation of another organization's practices rarely produces comparable results.

Organizations must focus relentlessly on developing people, not just improving processes. The ultimate goal is not just better operations but better problem-solvers at every level. Investing in training, coaching, and mentoring enables everyone to contribute to improvement. Creating opportunities for people to learn by doing, guided by those with more experience, builds capabilities. The skills and knowledge of the people will ultimately determine performance, no matter how sophisticated the technical systems become.

Embracing the power of small changes implemented immediately rather than waiting for perfect solutions or grand transformations accelerates progress. Starting with incremental improvements immediately allows them to compound over time. Too many organizations become paralyzed seeking comprehensive solutions to complex problems, when a series of small steps would move them steadily toward their goals. The bias for action distinguishes organizations that transform from those that merely talk about transformation.

Sustaining gains requires clear standards, visual management, and leadership accountability. Creating specific expectations for how work should be performed, making performance visible to all, and ensuring leaders at all levels fulfill their responsibilities for maintaining and improving systems prevents backsliding. Without these disciplined approaches to sustainability, improvements evaporate over time as people drift back toward familiar patterns or leave the organization, taking their knowledge with them.

Measuring what truly matters through metrics that reflect real value creation—safety, quality, delivery, service, employee engagement, cost—keeps organizations focused. Too many focus exclusively on financial outcomes, failing to recognize that these results flow from operational excellence rather than directly from management edicts. The metrics chosen highlight what is truly valued, so selecting them with care and reviewing them with consistency sends powerful signals.

Persisting through inevitable challenges is essential. The journey is not always easy or straightforward. Resistance will come from those comfortable with the status quo, setbacks will occur when improvements don't work as expected, and failures will test commitment. Learning from these experiences, adjusting approaches, and continuing to move forward distinguishes successful transformations. The organizations that experience breakthrough transformation are not those that avoid difficulties but those that respond to them with resilience and determination.

Celebrating successes along the way, recognizing and rewarding the contributions that make them possible, builds momentum and reinforces the culture of improvement. Making heroes of those who identify problems rather than hide them, who suggest improvements rather than defend the status quo, and who collaborate across boundaries rather than protect turf shapes culture more powerfully than any formal statement of values.

The journey of learning from extraordinary mentors like Bill Moffitt, Art Byrne, and Chihiro Nakao continues through the thousands of people on factory floors, in offices, and in boardrooms who have embraced this approach and made it their own. These practitioners demonstrate that the principles work not because of some mysterious Eastern philosophy but because they align with fundamental truths about how humans work together most effectively.

The true power of a holistic business system lies not in its technical elegance but in its human impact. When people feel respected, when they see their ideas implemented, when they take pride in delivering value to customers, they transform not just their work but themselves. They develop new capabilities, greater confidence, and deeper engagement. They bring their whole selves to work rather than merely complying with minimum requirements. This human transformation creates financial results that mechanistic approaches to improvement cannot match.

This transformation creates a living legacy that extends far beyond any individual leader or organization. It becomes a way of working and living that passes from person to person, organization to organization, generation to generation. The machine operator who sees a small improvement implemented becomes a problem-solver who teaches others. The supervisor who learns to listen rather than dictate becomes a coach who develops problem-solvers. The executive who goes to the workplace rather than summoning people to the boardroom models behaviors that reshape organizational culture.

The most profound lesson learned from three decades of practice is that this approach is not just a better way to run a business; it's a better way to be in the world. It embodies values that transcend business: respect for people, commitment to learning, dedication to excellence, and service to others. Organizations that embrace these principles create not just superior products and services but better places to work, stronger communities, and more sustainable societies.

The path of creating value is not a destination but a way of being. Each day presents new opportunities to observe, listen, and improve. Each interaction offers a chance to show respect and create value. Each problem contains the seeds of deeper understanding and better solutions. The journey never ends because excellence has no ceiling, and human potential has no limit.

The choice now lies before organizations and their leaders. Will they commit to this way of creating value? Will they be present, observe the work being done, and listen to those who do it? Will they relentlessly eliminate waste and focus on what truly matters to employees, customers, and society? The evidence is clear. The principles are proven. The potential is limitless. The time to start is now.

Leaders should reflect on what they've learned and consider what area in their organization could benefit most immediately from direct observation and listening. Identifying mentors or resources to support implementation, making small improvements immediately to demonstrate commitment, establishing metrics to measure progress, and sharing these principles with others extends the living legacy of creating value.

The greatest waste would be to read about this and do nothing. Taking action, starting small, persisting, and witnessing the power of a holistic business system will transform organizations, people, and leaders themselves. The journey of creating value never ends, but with each step, the path becomes clearer, the results more significant, and the impact more profound.

The way of creating value awaits those willing to commit to it. Together, organizations can build enterprises that deliver exceptional products and services, provide fulfilling work, generate sustainable profits, and contribute positively to society. The world needs more value creators, and the opportunity to become one begins with the decision to observe, listen, and improve.

About the Authors

John Rizzo is a seasoned business leader with over 30 years of experience in turnaround management and implementing holistic business systems across diverse industries. Throughout his career, he has led transformational change at multiple companies from executive positions, creating billions of dollars in value for employees, customers, and stakeholders.

Over the decades, he has facilitated or participated in more than 1,000 workshops across more than 50 companies and organizations, spanning manufacturing, healthcare, retail, nonprofit and numerous other sectors. He has tailored and applied holistic business systems to organizations ranging from small regional operations to global enterprises, consistently demonstrating that these principles work everywhere when properly implemented.

As the leader of Moffitt Consultants for a period in his career, he expanded his influence, guiding dozens of organizations through their own transformations. He had the privilege of learning directly from pioneers in the field, including Chihiro Nakao, Art Byrne, Yoshiki Iwata, Bill Moffitt, Bob Pentland, and Jim Cutler—mentors whose wisdom he has integrated into his own approach to creating value.

Throughout his career, Rizzo has maintained an unwavering commitment to developing people while improving processes. His approach balances technical excellence with profound respect for workers at all levels. He firmly believes that the best ideas often come from those closest to the work and that engaging employees in continuous improvement creates value that traditional top-down management approaches cannot match.

John Rizzo continues to advocate for a holistic approach to business that prioritizes creating value for all stakeholders—one that views respectful, sustainable improvement as both good business and the right way to operate in the world.

He is always willing to discuss creating value at john.rizzo@ moffittxl.com.

Tom Ehrenfeld has worked on more than 25 books, 11 of which have won the Shingo Publication Award. This includes popular books such as *The Gold Mine* by Michael and Freddy Balle, which topped sales of 75,000; *Lead with Respect* by Michael and Freddy Balle, which sold more than 50,000 units; and John Shook's *Managing to Learn*, which has to date sold more than 400,000 copies in a dozen languages. He has also worked as senior editor at the Lean Enterprise Institute for more than 20 years, helping found and lead its popular Lean Post, while conducting podcasts and leading webinars. He has worked on books by Art Byrne, Jim Womack, Jim Benson, Dan Markovitz, and Mark Graban.

Ehrenfeld has also worked as a writer and editor at magazines such as *Inc.* and *Harvard Business Review*, and has written more than 500 freelance business articles for *Inc.*, *HBR*, *Fortune*, *Business 2.0*, *The New York Times*, and many others. He wrote the popular weekly Just Managing column for the Industry Standard. He has worked with leading writers, including Amy Edmondson, Jim Collins, Peter Senge, and Jeff Liker.

Index

Page numbers followed by *f* refer to figures.